Stories From Home

Stories From Home

Memories of an Irish Childhood

Geraldine Noble Tyler

Copyright © 2008 by Geraldine Noble Tyler.

Library of Congress Control Number: 2008904670
ISBN: Hardcover   978-1-4363-4387-9
                   Softcover   978-1-4363-4386-2

All rights reserved. No part of this book may be reproduced or transmitted in any form or by any means, electronic or mechanical, including photocopying, recording, or by any information storage and retrieval system, without permission in writing from the copyright owner.

This book was printed in the United States of America.

To order additional copies of this book, contact:
Xlibris Corporation
1-888-795-4274
www.Xlibris.com
Orders@Xlibris.com

Contents

Acknowledgements 7

Chapter One: Lords and Ladies 11
Chapter Two: Aunt Sally 20
Chapter Three: The Quiet Man 26
Chapter Four: Friends 35
Chapter Five: A Gracious Lady 41
Chapter Six: Miss Alice Pierce 47
Chapter Seven: The Farm 52
Chapter Eight: Miss Vivienne Noble 56
Chapter Nine: The Sea 65
Chapter Ten: Aunts, Uncles, and a Stepmother 71
Chapter Eleven: Shadows 79
Chapter Twelve: Ruth 86
Chapter Thirteen: The Little Blue Car 90
Chapter Fourteen: Transitions 97
Chapter Fifteen: The Dances 105
Chapter Sixteen: Belfast 113
Chapter Seventeen: Escape from Rathcoole 121
Chapter Eighteen: Going To America 129

Epilogue 137

ACKNOWLEDGEMENTS

I have always wondered why so many Oscar winners spend the majority of their acceptance speech thanking everyone who was even remotely connected with their performance. I never understood why they thanked their spouse, their mother, their hairdresser, a plethora of family members, and so many people seemingly on the periphery of their lives. After all, they had won the award on the merit of their own acting.

Until I wrote this book.

It is true that these are my personal memories; that I organized the book and that I alone wrote it; that I spent endless hours staring at a computer screen wrestling with both the good and bad memories while struggling to recount them in an honest and entertaining way. However, I confess that the construction of this book was anything but insular. So many people living and dead contributed to my effort, and while writing it I was never alone. The ghosts of the past were always over my shoulder jogging my memory with both laughter and tears, while the living kept me grounded and on track.

So, I apologize to those Academy Award recipients whose speeches I never really appreciated, because I now understand why you thanked so many people. And in that light, I must express my own gratitude to a wide entourage of people who made this book possible.

To the colorful characters (friends, family and acquaintances) who inhabited my early life, and who created the foundation for this book.

My sister, Vivienne (Vivi) who read the first draft, and who graciously encouraged me to write it in my own style, saying, "It's your own personal memory, and you should write it just the way you remember it." She never suggested that I change anything that pertained to my memory of her.

My daughters, Kathleen and Tara, whose repeated response to my ramblings about growing up was, "Mom, you should write a book about it." And who then encouraged me in my endeavor.

My husband Gordon, whose love and constancy over the last thirty-five years has been an invaluable support.

My faithful friend Hilary, who filled in the gaps and jogged my memory when it flagged.

My Uncle Vivian, who so generously shared his memories of my father and their youth together.

My peers at Toastmasters, who responded so positively to some of the chapters that I condensed and presented as speeches.

Mike Foley, editor, whose advice and emotional support was a major factor in the completion of the book.

Dr. Margaret Doane, Professor of English Literature at California State University, San Bernardino, who first planted and then supported the idea that I indeed had writing ability.

David Vanderzell, owner of the beautiful D & D's Ballroom. When I despaired about being "too tall and too clumsy," he swept aside my doubts and managed to mould me into an acceptable ballroom dancer—a stark contrast to my humorously awkward beginnings portrayed in Chapter Fifteen.

Elvia Gomez, dance instructor extraordinaire, who instilled the concept of joy into the otherwise technical discipline of dancing. It was a lesson that spilled over into real life.

My granddaughter Kaitlyn and grandson Ian, who may someday read this book and marvel how we lived back then, before the advent of television, the Internet, iPods, and cell phones. Because they have brought such joy into our lives, and because I love them as only a grandmother can.

My appreciation and gratitude to all of you.

"Every man's memory is his own private literature."

Aldous Leonard Huxley.

CHAPTER ONE

Lords and Ladies

When I first came to America, I was surprised to find the complete absence of a class system. College students waited on tables in restaurants, rich people drove around in jalopies, the middle-class took expensive vacations, and accents never betrayed social standing. There was no nobility to speak of, and I was surprised to find that some of this country's presidents had actually emerged from humble origins.

The disappearance of rigid class barriers was at first disconcerting. For though class structures are restrictive, they also create an implacable sense of identity. Bereft of this security, for a long time I felt vulnerable and adrift.

However, I did eventually come to appreciate, and even embrace, this new freedom.

My childhood was unique. An Irish childhood. A wonderful adventure played out against the backdrop of an imposing manor house nestled within the parklands and gardens of a grand country estate. The estate hugs the eastern coastline of the Ards Peninsula and is situated adjacent to the sleepy coastal village of Ballywalter. It was to this childhood paradise that my father, worried about my mother's poor health, brought my mother and my sister, Vivienne, to live in 1939. Two years later, I made an enthusiastic entrance into the world. I was, by all accounts, an exceptionally happy child whose nickname soon became—Sunshine.

My father had been anxious to move my mother away from the city and into the clean country air, and it was this concern that prompted him to accept the position of electrical engineer at Lord Dunleath's large country estate. The estate consisted of a grand Manor House, walled parklands and gardens, and surrounding farm lands. My father's duties were to ensure the smooth operation of the large gas-generating engine that provided electricity for the great manor house, the employees' homes, and the buildings at the estate farm. A master mechanic, he was also responsible for the servicing and maintenance of the Lord's small fleet of limousines.

As befitting daddy's rank in the hierarchy of estate staff, he had been assigned a comfortable two-storied stucco home with a detached wooden garage. A carved stone urn decorated the front steps of the house, and a line of fragrant white hedge roses lined the southern side of the house. A small front lawn sported a plump red rose bush, and a long laurel hedge provided privacy for the back garden.

When I was growing up, the then Lord Dunleath was a middle-aged, courteous, white-haired gentleman of the old school with only one child, a son, Henry, who would inherit the estate upon his death. During the First World War, Lord Dunleath's brother, Edward, an officer with the Irish Guards, had been killed at Ypres in 1915, and Lord Dunleath, himself, had been badly wounded and awarded the Distinguished Service Order for valor.

In 1931 when his father died, he inherited the estate, and enthusiastically carried on the tradition of enhancing the woods and parklands that comprised the property. The Lord was an avid horticulturalist, and although there was already a head gardener and gardening staff in place, he took a keen personal interest in the extensive flora and fauna that his mother had imported to landscape the estate. It was not unusual for us to round a corner and come upon him, leaning heavily on a gold-tipped walking stick as he examined the towering rows of pink, red and white rhododendrons that lined the avenue up to the manor house. Sometimes, when my sister and I walked home through the estate from the village school, we would come upon him and his ever-present, faithful black dog, as he stood immersed in semi-circle of the discarded blue blossoms that he had just pinched back from the huge hydrangea bush beside the manicured croquet lawn. He often nodded and said, "Hello" to us, however, I was always awed by his presence because, not only was he so distinguished looking, but we had been taught to show respect for his position as Lord of the Manor. His acknowledgement of us was a gracious gesture from the "Great Lord" to his employee's children, and while I hung shyly back, my self-assured sister would acknowledge him with a polite, "Good Afternoon."

Lord Dunleath always dressed in accordance with his station, and even for his gardening forays appeared nattily attired in brown plus-four trousers tucked neatly into knee length socks. With a rustic tweed jacket to complete the effect, he presented the image of a quintessential country gentleman.

Each evening, in accordance with his aristocratic standing, and regardless of whether the family was entertaining, he dined formally dressed in the requisite dinner jacket. For Lord Dunleath, it was an engrained tradition and one to which he strictly adhered until his death in 1956. His wife, Lady Dunleath was an attractive, but somewhat haughty, patrician lady with a pencil thin figure, and a propensity for dark coats with fox-fur collars. She was formerly Henrietta D'Arcy, the daughter of the Archbishop of Armagh, high Prelate of the Church of Ireland; and when Henrietta D'Arcy married Lord Dunleath, she became a force to be reckoned with. She would have been in her mid-forties when I was growing up. We were all afraid of her, because at times, she could have a sharp tongue, and she kept a close eye on the manor house servants and the employees and their families who lived and worked on their large private estate and surrounding farm-lands. The farm had a large dairy herd, and once, when the wife of one of the men who worked in the milking shed came home from hospital with her tenth child, Lady Dunleath appeared at the door with a present for the baby. During the course of the visit, the new mother was politely asked, "Don't you think you have enough children now?" It was Lady Dunleath's way of saying, "You really don't need any more children. Time to stop"

As with many of the Great Homes, our Manor House had its own library, and Lady Dunleath would often read there by the fireside. If the fire should wane, she would ring the bell-pulley for a servant to come all the way from the Servant's Wing at the far end of the house simply to replenish the fire with a shovel of coal from the polished brass coal-scuttle that was sitting on the hearth—not eighteen inches away from her feet. That was Lady Dunleath, and she wore the mantle of aristocracy as if she had been born into it.

Often on Sunday, my sister and I and our friend, Hilary, would walk the mile and a half through the estate, out the lodge gates on the far side, and down past the village to the big stone Church of Ireland. The Church stood on a grassy bank overlooking the Irish Sea, and it was the same church that Lord and Lady Dunleath attended. After the service, we would usually be all the way back up through the village, and starting out through the estate by the time the Lord and Lady caught up with us. Lady Dunleath, probably feeling magnanimous, having listened to Sunday sermons about the "milk of human kindness," would sometimes have the chauffeur stop the yellow Rolls Royce, get out, and open the back door. She would then call out imperiously, "Get in children," and my sister, Hilary and I would clamber into the rear seat and be driven home in style, full of our own importance and feeling like royalty itself, because back then in the rural Irish environment of the 1940s and 1950s, the only people who had cars were the country doctor, the ministers and a few of the rich farmers. My father's hobby was motorcycles. He had two Nortons that he raced, and a big BSA with a sidecar, but riding around in a sidecar was not like being driven home in plush style with the nobility.

One Sunday, however, when Lady Dunleath stopped the car and called out, "Get in children," Hilary jumped into the back seat, but my sister stepped in front of me, looked Lady Dunleath in the eye and said haughtily, "No thank you. We prefer to walk. Come along Geraldine." And I, who always did what my sister told me, trotted obediently along beside her and gazed longingly at the big back shiny sedan as it went off down the road, over the old stone bridge and disappeared around the corner, ferrying the astonished Hilary home.

My disappointment stemmed from the fact that I loved to ride in the Lord Dunleath's Rolls Royce, because it made me feel like Cinderella going to the Ball in her gleaming coach drawn by prancing white horses. However, I looked up to my sister in everything, and it never occurred to me to question her authority.

Meanwhile, Hilary's amazement sprung from the fact that one simply did not refuse a command from the aristocracy. To her credit, Lady Dunleath kept stopping the car and offering us lifts home, which my sister, according to her immediate inclination, either graciously accepted or politely refused. To my knowledge, Lady Dunleath never said anything about it to my father, and I suspect she was secretly amused by the free-spirited little Miss. Noble, and may even have admired my sister's self-assurance, for, though she was just a little snippet of a girl, my sister was simply not intimidated by Manor Houses, luxurious limousines or aristocratic titles. In retrospect, I believe Lady Dunleath's amused tolerance of my sister's whims indicates that there was indeed a softer side lurking behind her granite exterior.

The Lady was fond of riding and had her own groom, Mr. Lilly, who lived in the lodge-house inside the tall wrought-iron gates that guarded the west entrance to the estate. One spring she organized and led a foxhunt for their extended family and circle of acquaintances. Between the estate-park and the farmlands, there was ample opportunity and space to flush some unsuspecting fox from its lair and chase the poor animal to exhaustion. As they started out, a long gaggle of red-coated riders trailing a pack of yelping hounds trotted in a dignified line right past our garden gate. Once past the house, they spread out across the fields and cantered in a staggered zigzag until they disappeared beyond the rise. Though they were out of sight, for a long time we could hear the faint braying of the hunting horns drifting back sporadically on the misty morning air. In those days, before the strident voices of the animal-rights activists were raised, the foxhunt was an established tradition among the landed gentry.

As members of the Northern Ireland aristocracy, the Dunleath family was closely associated with the British crown, and Lord Dunleath was a member of the British Parliament's House of Lords. In 1953 when King George died, his daughter Princess Elizabeth was crowned Queen in a glittering spectacle. Since Lord and Lady Dunleath were peers of the realm, they traveled to London for the event. After they returned, the estate workers and their children were invited to view their coronation robes. Kitty Magee, one of the maids, escorted us in shifts up one of the back staircases to a second floor anti-chamber where the robes they had worn hung in purple and ermine splendor. Kitty was quite a gracious person herself, and I suspect that being exposed every day to fine living had probably blunted her awe of opulence. Still, in her usual gentle way she agreed with our impressionable comments.

"Aye indeed," she would concur in her soft voice as the various spectators expressed their admiration. "They are lovely. And can you imagine what it must have looked liked in Westminster Abbey with hundreds of Lords and Ladies all wearing robes and coronets just like these." We were not allowed to touch anything, but I wanted to reach out and run my fingers over the beautiful smooth, velvety material, so unlike our cotton dresses and woolen sweaters. While Kitty may have been secretly amused by our, "oohs, and "aahs" for me the viewing of the robes was a visceral and aesthetic experience that drove home a strong association with the English throne and all things British. And, while I have retained my love of simple living, I believe that it was the stark contrast between this elegant world and our more homespun existence that made such an impression on me and cemented my appreciation, albeit it from afar, of Stately Homes and gracious living.

Back then, the big gentry-owned estates were communities unto themselves. At Ballywalter Park, the official name for Lord Dunleath's estate, the household staff resided in the servant's quarters within the great mansion. Some of the farm workers and gardeners lived in the nearby village. However, most of employees either occupied the several gatehouses that punctuated the stone walls encircling the estate proper, or were provided homes on the adjacent Park farmlands.

The children of the estate workers who lived on Lord Dunleath's farmland were as a matter of policy allowed entrance to the "Park" at all times. The walk to the village school was cut in half if we went through the walled estate. We took the gravel paths and manicured verges for granted, and would often vary our routes, in conjunction with the seasons, to enhance our trips. In the spring, carpets of bluebells transformed the woods over by the Gamekeeper's cottage into an enchanted forest. Although swampy in places, there was enough of a path so that we could squeeze through the thick underbrush.

The woods were always alive with mysterious rustlings, and although in my rational mind I knew they were just the sounds of rabbits darting in and out between the ferns and birds flitting between the trees, the romantic in me attached some vague mystical importance to the woods and their unseen occupants. Perhaps what I felt was some vague inherited association with my Celtic ancestors who placed a spiritual importance on their environment, and it was certainly more intuitive than rational.

In autumn we would sometimes circle over by the Head Gardener, Mr. Campbell's, two-storied Tudor house. There, the ferns were so thick under the trees that they dragged at your ankles and slowed down your steps. We spent many summer evenings swinging on Ian Campbell's rope swing behind his fathers house, and it never mattered if you fell off because the blanket of ferns would cushion your fall.

Occasionally, we would go by the carriage-houses attached to the East Wing of the Manor mouse. They ringed a cobbled courtyard, a throwback to the days when house-drawn coaches ferried guests down from Belfast. Though the Rolls and the Bentley had long since replaced the carriages, the atmosphere whispered of an era when the estate had provided employment for the whole community. Back then ladies-maids, footmen, valets, cooks and butlers attended to the indoor needs of the family and their guests. Outside, a small army of grounds-keepers, gardeners, grooms and gamekeepers kept the parklands and gardens manicured and stocked with game.

After passing by the gray stone carriage-houses, we would cut across the meadow where the riding horses grazed. From there we could pick up the main path again over by the old Blunder Bridge. The carved stone bridge spanned a pool of moss-covered water. I used to love to stop and drop stones over the side, and would then watch the ripples grow wider and wider until they disappeared against the green banks. In this enchanted place, the walk to school never seemed long. At night time it was a different matter. In the country darkness, the bridge turned menacing, for there was a story that someone had been hanged on one of the surrounding trees, and I always rode my bicycle over it as quickly as I could.

The Dunleath mansion became a familiar landmark as I passed by each day on my way to school. Though a symbol of power and authority, the fact that we all simply referred to it as, "The Big House" made it less intimidating. I'm sure the Lord and Lady would not have been pleased to hear their palatial abode described in this way, however the label, once attached, remained solidly in place.

As the years went by, I developed a strong affection for the mansion with its elegant façade, enhanced as it was by its gleaming white Doric porch, Corinthian columns, and classic lines. A sweeping driveway and a short, intricately carved, stone-railing wall fronted the house. We were not permitted to pass by on the driveway. The workers going to the farm from the village, and the children of the estate employees on their way to the village school were relegated to a small path below the manicured croquet lawn that swept away from the front of the house to blend with the fields and woodlands beyond.

Going through the estate, we had to observe certain rules such as, "no talking or running" when we went by the manor. Lady Dunleath, who was familiar with all the employees and their children, spent many an afternoon seated at an upstairs window scanning the area with a pair of binoculars. She was determined that no unsolicited entrant should trespass on her private property. And, if one of us had the impertinence to bring a village friend through the estate, she would raise the window and call down to us, demanding in clipped tones that the interloper must identify himself. Since all of us (except my sister, Vivienne) were scared of her to start with, this strategy effectively halted any unauthorized traffic through the estate. None of us was willing to risk being chastised by an irate Lady Dunleath.

Unfortunately, at that time I was growing at an unprecedented rate, and being clumsiness personified, would consistently stumble and fall, skinning my knees. This always happened on the gravel path by the crocus beds, just as we were approaching the "Big House." My friend, Hilary, became quite skilled at clamping her hand over my mouth, just in time to catch the first wail, while hissing in my ear, "Whist now, we'll none of us be allowed to come through the park any more if the Lady hears ye." Still, good fortune was always on my side, and none of my tripping occurred when Lady Dunleath was installed in her sentinel position, guarding the grounds from village invaders. Still, for two years I had a permanent bandage on my right knee, and my constant stumblings gave me a reputation for clumsiness.

Behind the mansion, a large domed glass observatory, housing an aromatic array of exotic flora and fauna, overlooked a wide sweeping lawn and softly shaded rock garden. Beyond, in a large kitchen garden with tall sheltering walls, the head gardener oversaw a small staff that tended the fruit trees, strawberry beds, hot houses, and extensive vegetable crop. This market garden provided produce for the manor's kitchen, and the excess was sold commercially to the local Greengrocers shops.

Though the Lord was a benign and considerate employer, we never forgot our place. However, he and his son, Henry, who later inherited the title, were singularly humane men. They both shared an intense love of their lands, and an uncommon respect for the workers who not only maintained them, but also considered the estate their home.

This consideration surfaced again in 1954. When Henry turned twenty-one, Lord and Lady Dunleath hired a live band, and the main hall was transformed into a dance floor for his coming-of-age party. In a magnanimous gesture, they gave permission for the estate employees to watch the festivities from the overhead balcony.

"Mr. Henry," as we called him, spent part of the year away at Eton, and Cambridge College in England. When he came home for the holidays, he would shun the Bentley, and roar around the countryside in a little sports car. If he passed us while we were walking down the road, he always stopped to give us a lift to the village. Mr. Henry wore a leather jacket, had sleeked-back dark hair, and he smoked cigarettes, and I thought he cut quite a dashing figure. I was thrilled with the news that we would be allowed to witness his party, albeit from afar.

On the evening in question we gathered to discreetly view the dance. True to form however, I became so enchanted by the glittering sight below that I ended up hanging over the banister for a better look, while Daddy whispered in my ear, "Get back, Geraldine or they'll all see you." However, below us, the white-gowned ladies and the men in their handsome tuxedos were far too involved in their waltzes and jitterbugging to cast even a random glance towards the great split-staircase or the intricately carved ceiling above. I was mesmerized by the flash of the swirling white skirts and the soar and dip of the music. It was a magical sight for an impressionable twelve-year-old, and was yet another example of our exposure to this elegant and privileged world.

Growing up at Ballywalter Park, my sister and I were fortunate to have been privy to the "upstairs" life of the gentry. It was an exposure that established in me a life-long appreciation for the world of the aristocracy. However, it was the wonderful array of colorful characters among the servants of the "downstairs" world of the manor house, and the village folk who tended the extensive gardens and estate farmlands that provided such an interesting and eclectic childhood. And then, juxtaposed against this kaleidoscope of lords and ladies, friends and acquaintances was . . . my family.

Our house at the Estate

Ballywalter

CHAPTER TWO

Aunt Sally

When I was seven, I fell in love. One afternoon, Aunt Sally and I had walked to the village and as we were passing Mr. Balmers' shop on the corner of Post Office Hill, I happened to glance through the window. Oh my goodness. There he was. The sight of him stopped me dead in my tracks. He was wearing a red bow tie with a blue and white spotted, waistcoat, and his amber-flecked brown eyes gazed knowingly at me through the glass. "I am here for only you," was the message they transmitted through the clear window. He was the most handsome teddy bear I had ever seen. I turned to Aunt Sally and uncharacteristically demanded, "Buy me that bear."

However, this was an era where, outside special occasions, children's demands for playthings were usually ignored and considered self-indulgent, and, true to form, Aunt Sally ignored my pleadings.

All evening I worried that someone would buy that bear that I knew had been created just for me. The next day, Aunt Sally and I returned to the village. On our arrival, the first thing she did was to march defiantly into Mr. Balmer's shop, buy the bear and hand him to me. I was elated. But why did Aunt Sally defy the status quo? It was for no other reason than she was intrinsically kind, and always responded to what she perceived as a genuine need.

When I immigrated to America eleven years later, I left my bear behind; after all I was beginning a new life, and I hoped it would be a fresh start for me. Now, all these years later, I wish I had taken him with me, even though he was battered and the worse for wear, with the stuffing coming out from under one arm and one of his beautiful brown *eyes missing. But, he was my constant companion, he slept on my bed every night, and I loved him. How could I have left him lying on the top shelf of a dark closet, abandoned, never to see me again?*

My sister, Vivienne, and I had the unique distinction of being the only children at Ballywalter Primary School without a mother. I was just a baby when, at the ridiculously young age of twenty-nine, my mother, Catherine, died. She had, after a long struggle with her health, died of complications from pneumonia. It was only a scant two years later that antibiotics became available, and so many times I have thought, *If only, if only they had been developed sooner* . . . . When my mother took ill, daddy's sister, our Aunt Sally came to take care of us. In retrospect she could probably have been considered, "a bit of a character," but a kinder person had never been born. She had a particular affection for young children and old folk, and she was very good to us. It was not until much later that, as an adult myself, I realized how lucky we were to have had her, and what a sacrifice she made on our behalf.

She was daddy's only sister. As a young woman, she had gone off to England and married an English army officer. She liked England. Compared to the rather restrictive society in Northern Ireland, England must have seemed very glamorous and exciting. Over there, the entire country did not shut down on Sundays, the way it did at home, with no shops open and no entertainment available.

We spent our Sundays going for long country walks and waiting for the day to be over. On Monday, all the busses would be running once more, and everything would be back to normal. Mr. Fowler, the village Newsagent, would reopen his shop, and Sammy Reagan would be behind the counter in his grocery store, selling provisions to the village customers. You would be able to have your prescription filled at the Mr. McClatchy's, whose chemist shop always smelled like of mixture of antiseptic and perfume, or you would again be able to buy an ice cream at the Ardmore café. On Sundays the country shut down completely, and the only institutions that were open were the churches. In contrast, across the Irish Sea in England, everything was open on Sunday, and there were dances, artistic events, military clubs and concerts to attend. For Aunt Sally, going to England must have felt like being set free, and no wonder she never intended to come back to Ireland.

However, she did come back to take care of us. She left England, and all she had there, to bury herself in the country with us, a mile from the nearest village, where the only musical sounds were the cawing of the crows in the tree-tops, the occasional lowing of the cows on their way to the milking sheds, and the wind rustling through the tree-tops. When she came to live with us, her husband, our Uncle Jim, was serving with one of the various military campaigns of the time. When the war was over, she did not leave us to go back to England for I was only four years old, and my sister, Vivienne, just six, and there was still no one else to take care of us. Instead, Uncle Jim would come over to Ireland on his various leaves. Uncle Jim was a genial teddy bear of a man with a soft, cultured English accent, and we looked forward to his visits because he always brought us presents. One year it was a badminton set, and another time, he gave each of us a kaleidoscope. I was mesmerized by the shifting shapes and colors that would metamorphose with just a twist of the wrist. Sometimes when he came, we would take the bus to Belfast. Living in the country as we did, it was a particular treat to experience the bustling, vibrant energy of a big city. When he went back to England, he took his special magic with him, and I missed him and the excitement he brought to our lives.

Back in those days, life was not easy for women. All the clothes had to be washed by hand and hung outside on the clothes to dry, or more likely draped over chairs by the fireside. Every house had an outdoor line and an indoor drying rack. In that cool, damp climate, before the advent of clothes dryers, it was a constant struggle to coax the moisture out of newly washed garments. At any given time, except perhaps in the dead of summer, you could walk into any house and seen steam rising from some piece of the washing that would be drying over a chair by the open fire. There were no vacuum cleaners or microwave ovens. Everything was cooked on the kitchen range. All the warm water for the house was heated in a cistern connected to the back of the all-purpose stove. And although it seems barbaric in this day and age, back then we only took a bath once a week—on Saturday night, so we would be clean for church the next day. During the week we would just wash at the bathroom sink.

Back then, the toilets were not part of the bathroom, and our toilet, although joined to the regular plumbing, was in an attached extension outside the house proper. To get to it, we had to exit the house and cross an outdoor room. In the winter, it was extremely chilly, and also drafty, and we all made use of the standard chamber pot, tucked inconspicuously under each bed. Nobody wanted to climb down the stairs at night to venture out into that unheated toilet.

One morning, while carrying my half-full pot down the stairs in the morning, I slipped, tumbled down the stairs, and the chamber pot flew out of my hands, spilling its disagreeable contents all over the front hall floor. I wasn't hurt, but sat on the floor in the middle of the puddle my fall had produced, crying as though the world had come to an end. Aunt Sally was nonplussed by the accident, fussed over me to make sure I was all right, and stoically cleaned up my liquid accident. Never once did she admonish me for being clumsy. In retrospect she hardly ever scolded either of us for anything and I think we both took her kindness for granted.

Although she managed well enough, Aunt Sally never seemed to fit into this rural life. Living in England had changed her and she had become comfortable with some of the practices that were still frowned upon in the comparatively restrictive Northern Ireland society. For one thing, she dyed her hair, and there was nothing subtle about the flaming red color she chose. She wore dark red lipstick, and had silk scarves and jewelry. Vivienne and I never tired of fingering her trinkets. My favorite was a ring with a large pale turquoise stone that changed shades of color when it was turned in the light. She had an ivory necklace carved in the shape of elephants that were connected to each other in tail-to-trunk mode—imprisoned forever in an endless march around my aunt's neck. And she smoked—in public. She always seemed to have money, and it was she, not Daddy, who bought most of our clothes.

Every summer, when Daddy took his two weeks vacation and went back down to the South of Ireland where they had both grown up, Aunt Sally took us up the coast to either Millisle or Donaghadee. In Millisle, we stayed with a lady who had a cottage at the end of a low lane with grassy banks on each side that were strewn with wild blackberry brambles. The cottage had a Dutch Door and I was fascinated by the fact that the top half of the door could open, while the bottom half stayed closed—and vice versa. In Donaghadee, we stayed at a hotel, and every day Vivi and I would go down to the harbor to watch the afternoon puppet show. We loved the puppet shows and all the children would laugh and clap as Punch and Judy and the blue-coated policeman cavorted through their scenes. Today, some of the puppet shows would probably be rated PG13 for violet content, but we all knew that it was make-believe and nothing to do with our ordinary lives.

When I was about eight, Aunt Sally opened a little shop in Ballyhalbert, the next costal village, about four miles down the coast. It was in the middle of a row of terraced houses. She sold sewing thread, stationary supplies and odds and ends. One cold blustery Saturday, she took us with her on the bus, and we spent the afternoon sitting behind the counter waiting for customers, but the only people to come in were an old lady with black hairs growing out of a mole on the side of her face, and a man with no nose. Aunt Sally told us afterwards that it had been blown off in the war. There were holes in his face where his nose should have been. I was horrified, but Vivienne, the future nurse, was un-phased by his appearance.

Soon after that Aunt Sally gave up the shop, and perhaps it was just her way of rising above the drudgery of being a just a housekeeper, especially after her more exciting life in England. She had been a champion swimmer in her day, and at one time had aspirations to swim the English Channel. Even though she was in her early forties when she was with us, she still braved the ice-cold wintry waters of Ballyhalbert Harbor for an occasional swim.

She was the kindest person I have ever known, and she would literally give away everything she had to people in need. She seemed to have a homing instinct for people in need, and there were a couple of families that she took on as personal project, giving emotional support and practical assistance in the form of clothing and food. Once in a while, she would take us to one of these homes. They were invariably bursting with children, and reeking with the smell of soaked diapers waiting to be washed. All diapers back then were cloth, and had to be washed by hand, and hung on racks to dry. Although the plastic diapers of today are not environmentally friendly, I believe that the mothers of that time would have been ecstatic at such a luxury. At the time, I did not appreciate her altruistic tendencies and I was always glad to get back to our own house with its lace-curtained, carpeted sitting room, polished piano and comfortable armchairs.

Aunt Sally could never resist children, and handed out a fortune in pennies so the "little one" could buy sweets or an ice cream. She encouraged me too, because I loved to dance and she would laugh and applaud and make me feel as though I was special.

One day when I was ten, I came home from school and she was not there.

"Where's Aunt Sally? I asked Vivienne.

She's gone," my sister replied.

"Gone where?" I asked in bewilderment for she was always there when we came home from school.

"I don't know. She packed her suitcase and left," said my sister.

The floor opened and I fell into some deep dark place. Without a word, Aunt Sally, the only mother I had ever known, had abandoned us. Was it my fault? Did I do something wrong? How could she just leave me—without a word? Was I so unimportant to her? At that moment the suspicion that I was unlovable was planted in some deep level of my psyche. That feeling and the deep void her departure left has stayed with me all throughout my life.

A year later Aunt Sally contacted us with the story of why she had left. Uncle Jim was divorcing her. If she had just told us that she was gong to leave, and why, instead of just disappearing, I'm sure it would have minimized the impact, and I would not been so angry at being abandoned. However, I expect at that moment she was too immersed in her own pain to consider how devastating her departure might have been to us.

However, Aunt Sally did leave. And, she never came back.

Aunt Sally

CHAPTER THREE

The Quiet Man

On one of the rare occasions when my father actually said more than a few words to me, he told me about his encounter with the train. One night when he was fifteen, he went out to the railroad tracks that skirted the small town where he lived. The evening train came by at approximately eight o'clock, at a time when the tracks would be shrouded in winter darkness. He eased himself down between the rails until he was lying as flat as he possibly could.

Then, when the great steam engine and carriages thundered over him, and the ground shook, my father closed his eyes and shouted a continuous, "Aaaah" at the top of his lungs until the train had passed over.

I was astounded.

"Why did you do that, daddy?" I asked, trying to imagine my somber, withdrawn father in the role of an exuberant, risk-taking youth.

"Well, I just wanted to see what would happen," was his response. "When the train passed by, I got up and walked home."

"But, did you tell anyone what you had done?" was my awe-struck response, for I was a timid ten at the time, and not possessed of the kind of courage that would induce me to risk my life, no matter what kind of thrill it would evoke.

"No," he replied, "Sure, I was smart enough not to tell anyone I had done such a foolish thing."

"But why, why did you do it?" I persisted, still struggling with the conflicting images of my father as a high-spirited, fun-loving youth, and the sad, silent man he had become.

He shrugged. "Sure it was just for the adventure," he replied.

My father was born on a Wednesday. According to the old superstitious poem we used to recite, Wednesday's child is "full of woe." By the time my sister and I had come to know him, events in his life had transpired to change him from the headstrong youth who had defied the train into a quietly tragic figure.

I think my father was one of those men who should never marry. Had he not met my mother, I think he would have been happy to spend all his free time reading, playing the piano and his accordion, and tinkering with the 500 cc Norton motor bike that he entered every year in the local races. Every August, he went back to the South of Ireland where he grew up. After he and my mother were married, and before they had children, they rode his bike "Down South" together, when he shared all his childhood haunts with her. I think it was a testament as to how important that motorbike was to him that he had actually given it a name . . . and a woman's name at that. He called the bike Mary Ann. He also liked the name, Kathleen, and it was that name he bestowed on my mother, even though her real name was Catherine. Rather than be offended at this misuse of her baptized name, my mother thought it was a great compliment, and she even changed her name on all of her piano music. Catherine Mackay Marshall became Kathleen Noble. I'm sure those early days of his marriage were some of his happiest time.

My grandfather was a Head Constable in the Royal Irish Constabulary during one of the most turbulent times in Irish history, and during my father's teenage years, Ireland was waging a terrorist war to free Ireland from centuries of British rule. The Irish Constabulary with its close affiliation to England was comprised of native Irish officers, and the Police Force found itself caught dead in the middle of the strife.

In 1920 the politician, Eamon De Vilera, negotiated a highly unpopular peace treaty with the English government. As terms of the agreement, six counties in the North of Ireland were ceded to England to remain under English rule, while the rest of the country would become the Irish Free State. The treaty was hugely unpopular, and it plunged the country into civil war, resulting in even more strain on the Irish Police force.

At the time my grandfather was stationed in County Offaly in central Ireland. Because of his position as Head Constable, the family lived beside the police barracks, and as a youth my father spent a lot of his time at the station.

I can only remember two times that my father ever shared anything about his past with me, and because open communication with me was such a rarity, those two incidents are seared into my memory. The first time it was to tell me the train story. The second time, it was like a window opening into, not only his past, but also into his psyche. I don't remember what triggered this particular reminiscence as he and I sat alone at the kitchen table one evening, but it was evident to me, even at my young age, that the early exposure to violent death had affected him profoundly.

"It was a terrible time," he said. "Families were fighting to death among themselves over the treaty. Some were for it, others hated it. They were bringing the bodies in every day. The policemen would stretch them out in lines on the station floor and cover them up with sheets." He shook his head and hardened his jaw as though he still had to steel himself to get past the memory of it. It was the only time he spoke of it, and he never brought the subject up again.

He never ever talked about growing up. It was my Uncle Vivian, daddy's brother, who told me about my grandfather, the Head Constable, who had the impossible job of policing while the country was in turmoil. According to Uncle Vivian, grandfather was an easy-going, affable man with the love of a good story and a keen sense of humor.

My grandparent's wedding picture, which for years was buried in an obscure photograph album, shows a large, handsome man with a handlebar moustache standing beside a slender, elegant lady wearing a high-necked, brocade floor-length gown. One of her hands rests lightly on my grandfather's arm, while the other trails a cascading bouquet of white heather and roses. They had four children together. My father, William, who was the oldest, was followed by Aunt Sally, Uncle Sam and finally, Uncle Vivian. My grandmother died while my father was still a teenager, and my grandfather remarried a lady from the North of Ireland. They had three sons together and when my grandfather retired, he moved the family up to the North as his second wife had never been happy living in the South. It was a hard wrench for my father who had to leave all his friends and the country side that he loved. He never liked Northern Ireland, and his heart remained firmly in County Offaly where he had grown up. However Belfast offered more opportunity for a master mechanic and electrician than the less industrial South, and by the time he met and fell in love with my mother, his destiny was firmly planted in the North.

My father was already in his thirties when they were married, and was working for a large aircraft manufacturing company in Belfast. They settled down in Cherry Valley, and the following year my sister, Patricia, was born. It was the beginning of a period of blows from which I don't think my father ever recovered. One day when Patricia was just a toddler and my mother had gone into another room to fetch something, Patricia reached up and pulled down a saucepan full of water that was boiling on the stove. She was severely scalded. She was taken to hospital but her injuries were so catastrophic that she died the following day.

I remember my Aunt Violet telling me about my mother's reaction. "She was in shock," recalled Aunt Violet sadly. "She kept saying over and over again, "I have to wash my hair, I have to wash my hair." I suppose her mind, unable to cope with the horror of losing her child in such a terrible fashion, directed her to focus on some mundane task that would occupy her consciousness. I believe the psychologists call it "transference." Years later my sister and I, rummaging through all the old photographs in the big wooden chest in the walk-in closet at the top of the stairs, looked at photographs of Patricia, and wondered what it would have been like to have our sister with us. We mourned her death, and daddy never entered the closet that held the sad ghosts of the past.

Aunt Violet sometimes offered me little tit-bits of information about our mother. "She was so ethical," said Aunt Violet. "She literally could not tell a lie. If we wanted to jump over a wall to pick an apple from a private garden, she would never go, because she knew it was stealing." And, by all accounts, my mother was a lovely person—warm and affectionate.

My sister, Vivienne, was born in February of 1939. I'm sure her arrival helped fill the painful void caused by Patricia's death. However, by that time my mother's health was deteriorating. She contracted TB, and it was then that my father, concerned about her health, took the job with Lord Dunleath at his estate near the little coastal village of Ballywalter. Daddy was hopeful that the clean, county air would help her condition. I was born two years after my sister, Vivienne, however, by that time, the doctors had decided that my mother needed to spend time in a sanitarium in Belfast where she could have complete rest. It was then that our Aunt Sally came back from England to take care of my sister and myself. Unfortunately, the following year my mother contracted pneumonia and died. Never knowing my mother has left a void in my life that nothing has ever been able to quite fill. For a while, Aunt Sally was an excellent substitute and we were lucky to have her. However, I have often thought that if I were ever granted the three proverbial storybook wishes, the first one would be to meet and spend a day with my own mother—to make that connection, to tell her I love her, and to feel whole again. As a result of my own situation, I have an instant empathy for orphans who search futilely throughout their lives for their elusive identity; an identity that can only come from the parental connection.

After my mother died, my father drew back into himself. He found relief in his work, which he would extend into the after-hours by taking on electrical jobs for the local farmers, or tinkering with one of his three motorcycles. Back then, Motorbike racing was already an established sport. The two largest races were the North West 200 and the Carrowdore 100. Generally, the race would be ten or twenty laps, with each lap consisting of about ten miles of country roads, which would be cleared of traffic for the occasion. The Carrodore 100 actually skirted the north side of Ballywalter, coming down the coast and turning inland by the church at the north end of the village.

Vivi and I would watch for him behind the stubby stonewall that ringed the church rectory and graveyard. When he passed by, we would jump up and down waving and shouting, "Daddy, daddy!" however he was always intent on navigating the steep corner at high speed and he never saw us. He was a distinctive rider on his sleek, black Norton 500 c.c. motorbike. Because he had a handicap, he was always allowed to start first in the staggered field, and his bike sported a large black #1 painted on a white, oval sign to indicate his identity and the fact that he was the first-off in the field of riders. Years before, when he was riding his Norton on city streets, a taxicab made an illegal turn, and had broad-sided him. His leg was shattered and he spent the next year in a hospital bed. Surgery and a steel rod could not completely correct the damage, and he could never bend his leg again. My energetic father was not one to be deterred by his potentially restrictive situation. He improvised. He could still walk, albeit with a heavy limp. He found that he could still ride a bicycle by rotating the left pedal with his good leg, and when the right pedal came around he would slap it with his extended foot of his injured leg. For his motorbikes, he simply had the right foot-rest extended forward to accommodate his outstretched leg. He was active to the point of restlessness, and I think he was always trying to outrun his grief by continually staying busy.

Although my father had moved to the country for my mother's health, and, although he often pined for his boyhood haunts and the friends he had left in the South of Ireland, I think his job at Lord Dunleath's estate suited him much better than his job at the aircraft factory. He had relative freedom, going about the country estate with its gardens and park-like atmosphere as he ensured the smooth running of the estate's power supply. As a master mechanic, I think he enjoyed working on Lord Dunleath's cars and he was a great favorite of Lord Dunleath's son, Henry, who was a racing enthusiast and appreciated my father's skill and knowledge of all things electrical and mechanical. If anyone should ask, "Where is Mr. Noble?" the answer would invariably be, "He's under a car in the garage with Mr. Henry."

Daddy also had a garden, with apple trees, a damson tree, a large vegetable garden, and a glass-house for growing tomatoes. He enjoyed working in the garden during the summer months when the days were long and the sun didn't set until ten o'clock in the evening. Every year, he preserved jam, and I spend many summer afternoons in our garden picking blackcurrants, redcurrants and gooseberries for the jams he made that would often last us through the winter months. It was tedious work, and I spent as much time sitting on the little L-shaped sod wall with the giant sun-flower growing out of one side. I would watch the butterflies flitting about, and drink in the almost overpowering scent wafting from the bed of Sweet William planted by the glass-house.

My sister told me that he had strategically planted the rows of flowers outside the kitchen window so that they would bloom at different times so our mother would always have flowers to look at as she washed dishes or clothes at the kitchen sink.

At the end of the day, daddy would pay me a bright sixpence, and as soon as he handed it to me with a, "Here you are Geraldine," I was off on my bicycle racing down the estate road to the village to spend it on sweets at Mr. Fowler's newsagent shop.

I do remember the one time I saw him happy. Perhaps, because it was so out of character, that it has remained an entrenched memory.

When I was about seven, our Uncle Vivian, who spent his career with the Royal Air Force, his wife Aunt Angela and their little daughter Jane, came to visit. One evening, the adults disappeared into the sitting room and before long the sounds of daddy's piano accordion and the piano came drifting out into the kitchen were Vivi and I were getting ready for bed. When the door opened, and Aunt Sally came out to say goodnight, I had a glimpse into the room. It was all warmth and bright light and daddy was laughing and playing the accordion and everyone was talking. Seeing this happy side of my father actually startled me because he seemed like a different person. I think my father was very fond of my Uncle Vivian and we always received gifts from the various places where Uncle Vivian was stationed. My favorite was a glass replica of tree branches on which perched delicately colored butterflies. My Aunt Angela was a sweet lady who always showed a lot of interest in Vivi and myself, and she always made us feel important.

I don't actually remember my father talking much to our Aunt Sally and when she left abruptly, he never said a word to us about her. It was a terrible shock to me, and even after she wrote to us months later to tell us she had gone back to England because Uncle Jim was divorcing her, my childish anger over being abandoned lasted well into adulthood. I think my anger was exacerbated by the fact that her leaving us set into motion a sequence of events that eventually culminated in even more loss. I would, however, evoke my second storybook wish to be with her, and to tell her how much I appreciated everything that she did for us. I'm not sure she was ever thanked in her lifetime for her altruism on our behalf.

In the meantime, we took our lead from daddy's silence and we never talked about her after she left. I think it left both my sister and myself with the idea that one kept pain and loss inside, and that it was something that should never be shared with anyone else. It was almost as though, for daddy, Aunt Sally had never existed, even though she gave up her own life to take care of us for so long. How could he not have acknowledged her sacrifice?

For the next two years my sister, Vivienne, and I took care of ourselves. Aunt Sally began sending Vivienne and I pocket money on a regular basis—a fact that daddy pointedly ignored. The postman dropped the letters off at Mrs. Johnson's house at the end of the lane, and Mrs. Johnson would prop the envelopes up in her window, so that when we passed her house on our way home from school, we would know that Aunt Sally had written to us. Once a week, Daddy would go into Sammy Reagan's grocery store and order groceries for the week, and every Thursday afternoon Sammy would drive up the lane to our house in a trap pulled by his brown pony with the long black mane, and deliver the groceries, which consisted of ready-to eat item in cans. I think in those days Vivienne and I existed on bread, eggs, cheese, cereal, the occasional sausages Daddy would travel up to Newtownards to buy, and all the fresh produce from our garden. For some reason, he boycotted the Skillen Brothers butcher shop in the village square, and we never found out why he refused to set foot over their threshold. Back in those days, everything was fresh, and every day at school all the children were provided with a third of a pint of milk. I don't think this diet ever did us any harm for we were both healthy and never sick.

Every now and then, I would see Daddy looking at us with a worried look on his face. We were ten and twelve at the time, and neither of us had been taught to cook or do household chores, and we virtually lived by ourselves, as daddy was gone most of the time, even on weekends. It was during this time that I think he felt he would have to do something about the situation. And it was then that he met Mary, our future step-mother.

My Mother—Catherine Noble

My Father—William Noble

Grandfather and Grandmother Noble on their wedding day.

CHAPTER FOUR

Friends

Although I have developed a great affection for America, my adopted home, I do sometimes feel nostalgia for my spiritual home, Ireland. When this occurs, I call my friend, Hilary. It has been fifty years since I left Lord Dunleath's estate, and Hilary now lives in England.

When Hilary answers the phone, I always say, "Hello Hilary, it's me," and although it may have been a year, or even two or three years since I last rang her, and although I am calling out of the blue, Hilary, invariably, without missing a beat will immediately reply, "Och, Geraldine, it's you. How are you?"

She's my life-line to everything precious about my childhood. It's a bond I treasure.

Of all of the friends I have had at various times over the years, none remains as vividly entrenched in my memory as those friends from childhood. How lucky I was to have such interesting and diverse companions—pretty, brown-eyed Joan Foster who loved to laugh; blond, statuesque Hilary Reid who was an avid reader; and petite, curly-haired Ellie Chambers with the beautiful sapphire-blue eyes who was always ready for an adventure.

Joan Foster lived two fields away in a house appropriately called "Sandgate Cottage." The cottage sat at the bottom of a grassy hill, with a small plantation of Fir trees on three sides, and only a wall separating it from the shoreline beyond. The stone and slate wall had a wooden door in its center. To access the sea, one only had to go through the door and trudge down a deep, sandy path lined by grassy sand-dunes in order to exit onto the beach. Out on the shore about a half mile away to the left, the grey, village buildings etched the skyline, and to the right, a rocky promontory jutted into the sea, obscuring a view of the coastline to the south.

Joan lived in Sandgate Cottage with her mother, father and older sister Margaret. Although she was a year ahead of me in High School, we became quite good friends, and many Monday nights, we would ride our bikes into the village to see whatever new movie was showing at the newly-renovated movie house in the village square. When Joan and I were together, we became gigglers, and I can remember sitting on the bus going home from school one day, spending the entire half-hour trip doubled up with laughter over nothing in particular. Once, we went around the houses along the strand south of the village selling red poppies to make money for the War Veterans Homes, and we could hardly get through our introduction without giggling. "Would you like to donate something for the Veterans?" Joan would start out, straight-faced, her brown eyes serious."

But as soon as some flustered housewife would run to get a shilling to put into the can, Joan would double up with laughter, and could hardly contain herself as the lady would drop her coin, with a plop, into the can and accept the traditional red poppy to wear on her lapel—a symbol that she had donated to this worthy cause.

One night when riding home from the Monday night movies, we were laughing so hard that our handlebars became entangled and we went sprawling across the road. I was unhurt, however Joan had a large deep square-shaped scrape under her eyes, and as the wound healed, it formed a bumpy scab that Joan referred to as "apple crumble." Somehow the similarity to the crust of apple pudding seemed hilarious to her, and was indicative of her ability to see the humor in everything, no matter how unfortunate the circumstances.

She was good for me because I could sometimes be too serious, and she helped me to laugh at life. It was Joan's father whom I called, "Uncle John Foster," who taught me to ride my first bike, given to me by my friend, Hilary. Hilary donated her old bike to me after she acquired a new, technological masterpiece. Hilary's new bike actually had three-speeds; a bike that made pedaling around the country roads so much easier than my newly acquired, antique version. However, I was so thrilled to have wheeled transportation that I was forever grateful to Hilary for this precious gift.

The Reids lived in a long whitewashed cottage just inside the walled estate. The cottage was covered with Virginia Creeper, and in Autumn the vines turned the most glorious shades of red and gold, and when the sun bathed the cottage with late afternoon light, it was suddenly transformed into an enchanted, storybook cottage. Thick bushes of red and green Honeysuckle grew in clumps around one side of the house, and throughout the summer, the hum of bees flitting from one blossom to another created a buzzing chorus that droned through the lazy afternoon air.

When Mrs. Reid was a young girl, Lady Dunleath had hired her to work in the manor house nursery. Lord and Lady Dunleath had one child, a son named Henry, and in those days the gentry's children were raised by nannies. Mrs. Reid's duties were to help the head-nanny and to keep the young Master Henry amused. Because of her service to the family, Lord and Lady Dunleath had given her the estate cottage to live in indefinitely.

Mrs. Reid loved flowers and from January through December her living room would be decked with vases filled with either, snowdrops, bluebells, primroses, or whatever flowers were currently blooming in the surrounding woods. My friend Ellie and I spent many an afternoon hunting among the mossy banks in the woods in front of Mrs. Reid's house for bunches of yellow primroses to fill her glass vases. In summer Hilary, Ellie, Vivienne and I would make mud cakes in the back woods and decorate them with leaves and wild flower petals and Mrs. Reid would duly trudge up through the wood to judge the best adorned "cakes."

I loved the ice-cold water in the well in her back garden, and after a summer afternoon of creating fake culinary masterpieces, we were always appreciative of a glass of her refreshing well-water. Mrs. Reid, bless her, was always ready to serve anyone who needed a delightfully chilly beaker of chilly, delicious water, and she was never tired of hearing me exclaim, "Mrs. Reid, now that's the best water you could ever drink." There were no soft drinks back then and we even had to wait until we were twelve before we were allowed to drink tea. Milk and water were the liquid staples of the day.

We were so lucky because we could roam the fields and explore the woods to our heart's content, and we often ventured past the old pigeon house, where families of pigeons still made their homes in the cubby holes carved out in the now crumbling walls. On our longer forays, we would tramp down the still tree-canopied, dirt-packed road that wound from the gates on the west side of the estate towards the gravel path at the entrance to the Manor

House. This long-forgotten road was once the main route for the horse-drawn carriages that ferried guests and relatives down from Belfast to visit Lord and Lady Dunleath.

Wherever we were roaming on the estate, our unofficial reminder to go home came at 6 o'clock, when Tom Brown, who worked all day in the barnyard buildings, would ring the big tower bell in the lower courtyard. The bell could be heard all across the country side and it was the signal for the end of the workday for all the farm men.

Sometimes on summer nights, we would build a fire in a clearing in the woods in front of her house and roast potatoes. As the cooking potatoes spluttered in the flames, we would lie on our backs on the scattered pine needles, peer at the stars through the tree tops, and frighten ourselves with ghost stories. Luckily, Lord Dunleath never found out what we were doing in his precious woods, and clever Mrs. Reid always had a container of water handy in case a stirring ember sparked out of the safety zone.

Mrs. Reid had a white goose, Albert, and a black cat, Nero, who would follow us into the woods and stay by the fire. Mrs. Reid used to joke that, "It was just as well that we were living in a modern world, for in another time we would all, for sure, be burned as witches."

She was good to me and I never had to knock at her door, which was always unlocked. In those days, nobody ever locked their doors, and I could just walk in. "Och Geraldine," she would say, "How are you dear." She always made me welcome, and we spent all endless hours playing monopoly, or chatting to Kitty, who was Lady Dunleath's maid, and who would walk over from the Manor House on her evenings off.

My other friend, Ellie Chambers, lived with her mother and step-father, Joe Peak, and her younger half-sister Kathleen. Mrs. Peak, Ellie's mother, was very kind to me and every now and then she would cut my hair when it grew long enough to alter the short tomboy look that I favored.

Ellie's step-father, Joe, was the estate carpenter and a skilled gardener. His tomatoes, grown in a large glass-house, were the deepest shade of red. I used to like to go into his greenhouse and smell the rich loam and the pungent scent of tomato vines. One summer when my sister and I had climbed up onto one of the barnyard roofs, Ellie joined us and produced a bag of tomato sandwiches that her mother had made for us. And there we sat, basking in the warm summer sun and devoured every single sandwich in the bag. There is nothing quite like the taste of a sliced, hot-house tomato, sandwiched between two pieces of heavily buttered thick Ormeau Bakery bread, and every time

I eat a tomato today, I think of Ellie's summer afternoon sandwiches which, at the time tasted like a King's feast.

It was Ellie who first told me about the facts of life. It remains an entrenched vivid memory. I was twelve and we were pushing hard against the wind on our bikes as we were passing the War Memorial on the south side of the village. I'm not sure why Ellie picked such an unusual time to give me such important information, but I do remember being horrified, and from then on looking at her parents, and all other married couples, and struggling with the distasteful image of people engaged in such an intimate act.

"How can they do that?" I asked Ellie, who was a year older than me and who did not seem to share my reservations.

"Well they do," replied Ellie in a matter of fact tone. "You'll get used to the idea."

Of course, Ellie was right and my attitude changed as soon as I became interested in boys myself. But I can still remember the sting of the wind in my face, and in my peripheral vision, the statue of the uniformed World War I soldier posed, rifle in hand, atop the stone pillar that held the names of all the local men who had died fighting in both the World Wars.

As important as my friends were, it was their mothers who for years helped fill the deep void created by the absence of my own mother. Joan's mother, Mrs. Foster, always made me welcome and she had a good sense of humor. She was a secret smoker at a time when the sight of a woman smoking was deemed highly inappropriate. Any time there would be a knock on the door, she would rush to extinguish the forbidden cigarette and to frantically wave away the odor of smoke. This was always accomplished amid gales of laughter with Joan and I collapsing with a fit of the giggles.

In retrospect, I realize that I was a compulsive visitor who spent every moment I could away from our house. I was always in the fields or the barnyard with the farmhands, or at other people's houses. I also now understand that I was simply emulating my father, to whom being home meant facing the death of his young wife and little daughter, our sister Patricia. This catastrophic loss left him emotionally unable to interact with my sister, Vivienne, and myself. Since neither of us wanted to be in that empty house, Daddy's solution was to work endlessly, while I became a serial visitor. I relied on my friends and their families to take the place of my parents. They never disappointed me. Later, when I had to move away from my beloved home and friends, it was my Belfast relatives who took the edge off the deep void this loss created.

Mrs. Reid (left), Kitty (Lady Dunleath's maid), and Eleanor (Hillary's sister)

Hillary and her bicycle

CHAPTER FIVE

A Gracious Lady

> *I have always loved the story of Cinderella, perhaps because my favorite character from all of the childhood fairy tales is that of the Fairy Godmother. The Fairy Godmother was caring and protective, but most of all—magical. She plucked Cinderella from her existence of drudgery and loneliness and transported her into a glittering world of elegance. Most of all she loved Cinderella, wanted only the best for her, and was determined that she should prosper.*
>
> *Everybody should have such a fairy godmother.*

In the luck of life's draw, some children are fortunate enough to be presented with an adult ally; a magical mentor to guide and nurture. And indeed, my sister and I were lucky enough to have our own fairy godmother, who perhaps did not quite fit the fairy tale mould, but who nevertheless functioned beautifully in just that capacity.

Our fairy godmother was not the pink-cheeked, golden-haired, smiling deity fashioned in the world of storybooks. She was a tall, broad-shouldered woman, with white hair and glasses. Hampered by a degenerative form of rheumatoid arthritis, she moved about slowly with the aid of a sturdy wooden cane. In her heavy tweed skirt, and sensible black shoes, she exuded an aura of severity. But that was just the first impression.

When you talked to her, you began to notice a definite twinkle in her blue eyes, and that her hair was really more of a silvery-white than just plain white. When she was amused, her laughter sounded like the peal of Sunday bells. And then there was her name. Mrs. Grace Little.

Amazing Grace.

The Littles were our nearest neighbors. Mr. Little managed the estate farm, and his imposing stucco house stood, sentinel-like, on a rise that afforded its occupants a clear view of the barnyards, dairy, surrounding fields, and the farm employee's houses. From the attic, they could see over a row of distant trees to where the azure line of the Irish Sea etched the ocean horizon.

As Lord Dunleath's land steward, Mr. Little held an important rank in the hierarchy of estate employees. He was responsible for all the farm operations. It was a large farm with dairy herds, flocks of sheep, hens and pigs. There was also a large annual harvest of wheat, hay, potatoes—whatever crops were in rotation in any given year. Tractors and farm equipment had to be maintained, the carthorses shod and pampered, and of course he was always working with an eye towards that all-important bottom-line profit.

Since estate dwellings were relegated according to position, the land steward's house was, by design, an elegant building set on a manicured lawn and surrounded by a neat gravel path. There was a large drying green at the back of the house, and a clothesline that stretched the entire length of the grass. Mrs. Little adhered to a strict schedule. Monday was for washing and starching, and Tuesday was for the ironing.

She had a large flower and vegetable garden that was maintained by workers from the farm. Often in the summer when I came up to visit, she would be standing outside leaning on her cane chatting to the men. She always had a kind word for the farm employees, and they, with caps off and shirtsleeves rolled up, would rest their Wellington Boots on their spades and hoes and respectfully answer her inquiries about their families.

At the opposite end of the lawn, there was a tidy row of white bee hives. In summer, swathed in beekeeper's attire and limping heavily, she harvested the honey herself. The house and grounds were encircled with a clipped laurel hedge, and backed by a small copse of pine trees that served as shelter against the bitter winter winds.

She was friendly with my Aunt Sally. My aunt, being raised in a home where emphasis was placed on education and the arts, recognized in Grace a kindred spirit, for, when Grace was young and single, she had immigrated to Australia. In an era when women were expected to stay home and raise a family, she had opted to travel, and spent several years in Sydney working at a millinery shop.

She returned to Ireland where she married Mr. Little who had been recently widowed, and was left with four motherless children. She was a distant cousin of his dead wife, and it was not unheard of back then for a widower to remarry within the same family, especially if there were children involved. When I was growing up, there was only one son left at home. George was a tall, lean, fresh-faced fellow with sandy hair and a shy smile.

Each morning he walked down the hill and past our house on his way across the fields to Killyvolgan where he worked on the Little's own family farm. In the evening he would trudge back up the hill with the spring beaten out of his step from a hard day's labor on the land. Later on, he married and went to live at Killyvolgan, and I missed the comfortable routine of his greeting as he passed by.

Mrs. Little took a keen interest in our well-being. No doubt the fact that we were motherless evoked in her a particular sympathy. We were always welcome at her house and, by the time I was four years old, and Vivienne six, we were being issued regular invitations for afternoon tea. Hand in hand, my sister and I would walk up the road that cut through the field to her house. Aunt Sally always watched until we passed through Mrs. Little's iron-gate and disappeared behind the laurel hedge.

Often in early summer when we went to visit her, one of the farm men would be up there working in her garden, either weeding around the vegetables or tying her sweet pea onto stakes. She loved sweet pea and had entire rows of the pink, lavender and white flowers. Their scent was so fragrant that it would waft down the road to greet us long before we ever reached the gate.

She was always glad to see us.

"Och, look who's here," she would say by way of greeting. "Sure it's Vivienne and Geraldine up to visit." Living abroad had modified her accent, and given it a modulated undertone that sounded very sophisticated to us. Whether it was a formal invitation for tea, or one of the many times as I grew older after Aunt Sally left and I drifted up there by myself, her response was always the same. Not only did we feel welcome, she always managed to create the impression that our presence had somehow added luster to her day.

She used to call me "Sunshine." "Because you're like a wee ray of sunshine," she would say. It was a nickname that defied all reality. Although I did have a sunny disposition, it was often offset by a bad temper and an intractable stubborn streak. She called Vivienne, "Fairy." "For you're as delicate as a little elfin," she would say. And, it is true that Vivienne was as slender and graceful as anything that might emerge from the spirit world.

Even back in the early days when we were still small children, she always treated us with kindness and respect. The kindness is easy to understand for the Irish love their children, however the respect part was a different matter altogether. In an era when children were usually met on their own unsophisticated level, Mrs. Little never lowered her conversational standards simply because we were very young. Even at that early cognitive stage, we were receiving and storing the subconscious message that we were somehow special, and certainly more sophisticated than our peers at the village school.

Our afternoon teas simply cemented this impression. It wasn't like stopping at a friend's house where you might be offered a biscuit from the tin, and a drink of milk. This was a fully-fledged English afternoon high tea. Set with fine china, the heavy mahogany table in the parlor was covered with a white linen tablecloth. Our cups and saucers were decorated with dainty pink roses and trimmed in gold. The plates were so delicate that when you set your fork down, the china reverberated with a tinkling echo. Tea was brewed in a large country-cottage teapot covered with a hand crocheted cozy to keep it warm. Dainty tomato finger sandwiches were tastefully arranged on scalloped-edged plates. A three-tiered silver pastry dish held an assortment of crème-filled delicacies, and there was sure to be a plate of my favorite currant squares somewhere on the table. The piece de resistance was usually a hand-baked cake smothered in pure butter icing. Our silverware, polished every month by her maid Emily, was so clear that we were able to see our reflection in it. There was no mistaking the message that we were worth the best.

After tea, Vivienne and I would sit there in her parlor and talk to her. The conversations always revolved around us.

"Now tell me ladies," she would begin our after-tea conversation. "What lessons are you learning in school this week?" And Vivienne and I, who by now would be feeling like elegant sophisticates, would enthusiastically compete to impress her with our newfound knowledge. She would nod and smile and exclaim, "Indeed." or "Well done," when one of us ran flawlessly through our multiplication tables.

The room was west facing, and on clear days the sun picked up the scroll designs on the lace curtains and reflected them onto the roll-top writing desk. Surrounding us were the fruits of her artistic labor. Before her arthritic condition worsened, she was a prolific artist and accomplished needlewoman. Her delicate watercolors of the Irish landscape were aesthetically arranged around the room. Over the mantle hung an impressive portrait of highland deer, frozen in startled flight. I always had the uncanny feeling as they stared down on us with their wide brown eyes that they were somehow listening to our conversation. The fireplace-screen, decorated with a splash of embroidered red and pink flowers, infused the room with warmth and color. The frustration she must have felt in having her artistic talent stifled by her crippled hands was never voiced; though I'm sure she was pleased with our constant admiration for all the beautiful artwork she had created.

Those were enchanted afternoons made magical by the perfume of cut flowers in crystal vases, her golden-framed paintings, and our inclusion in the conversation of adult gods. And though at the time I was too young to fully comprehend its significance, I was vaguely aware that she was creating something special just for us, the two little Noble girls from down the road. Her validation of us, not as children, but as important human beings created a profound and enduring impression. The memory of those afternoons in her polished parlor, during which she treated us not as children but as important human beings, has been forever indelibly etched in my memory. And even to this day, I always drink my tea from a china cup; not just any cup—a fine china cup decorated with pink and red roses edged in gold trim that, when touched by a spoon, reverberates with an echo, a tinkling echo from that particular fairy-tale part of my past.

Mrs. Little (A Gracious Lady) and Mr. Little

Vivi and myself on our way to visit Mrs. Little

CHAPTER SIX

Miss Alice Pierce

I am a firm believer in the sentiment that, "Love sees with the heart, not the eyes," and this belief was recently reinforced during a transatlantic conversations with my childhood friend Hilary. We were talking about Miss Pierce the dairy maid at the estate when we were growing up, and my comment, "I thought she was so beautiful" slipped into the conversation.

There was a silence on the line.

"Miss Pierce," responded Hilary incredulously. "Miss Pierce!" she repeated. "Are we talking about the same Miss Pierce?"
"Yes," I said, somewhat surprised by her reaction.
"Sure Miss Pierce had a long face and a big nose. She was no beauty," said Hilary emphatically.
"But, I always thought she was lovely," I insisted, bewildered by Hilary's assessment.
"Oh no," replied Hilary. "She was no great shakes in the looks department." It was a frank appraisal which my sister later corroborated.

I was flabbergasted by these opinions that contradicted my memory of Miss Pierce. However, I realize that, what Miss Pierce really looked like is not important. The only thing that matters is that, to my child's eye, and in my adult memory, she was, and will forever remain . . . . beautiful.

Around 1949, the dairymaid at the farm left, and all the farm employees were abuzz with excitement over who the new dairymaid would be. The news filtered down that the new dairymaid would be a Miss Alice Pierce who would be coming to us from Lord Dunleath's cousin, Lord ONeill's estate away up in County Fermanagh. I was enchanted with Miss Pierce from the moment I laid eyes on her and she, in return, was always kindness itself to me.

As Lord Dunleath's employees were assigned houses according to their jobs, Miss Pierce was given the pink, two-storied brick house that was situated across from the dairy. The dairy was set just off the lane at the edge of one of many rolling fields of long, waving green grass. In this bucolic setting, the large herds of black and white Friesian cows roamed about, and obediently trotted back and forth to the farmyard twice a day for their milking.

From the outside, the dairy was a grey stone, rather gloomy, building. In contrast, the walls inside were covered from floor to ceiling with gleaming, white tiles. A ledge about two feet down from the ceiling ringed the room. On this ledge, designer plates in various pastel colors, interspaced between plates of the traditional blue willow pattern, stood upright along the entire four sides of room. It was a delicate, aesthetic touch that almost seemed incongruous because the dairy was a place of back-breaking hard work. Miss Pierce started at five in the morning and, after a two-hour break in the middle of the day, was there until after six in the evening.

Twice a day she bottled all the milk that was trundled over in big steel cans from the cow byre. The farm man who brought the milk would climb up a ladder at the side of the cooler which looked like an enormous glass wash board. When he emptied the contents of the can into a funnel at the top, the milk streamed down the grooved glass into a trough at the bottom, and from there into glass bottles that were hooked to the trough, and supported underneath by retracting pedals. As each bottle filled up, the dairy maid would release it and place it into a wire crate. Each crate held twelve bottles, and each bottle was hand-sealed with a silver aluminum top. When the crates were full of finished bottles, they were stacked in the corner. Twice a day she had to scour and sterilize all the stainless steel equipment that was used in the bottling process. It was hand-washed in stainless-steel sinks and then loaded into ovens where it was washed again and then sterilized. When the cycle was finished, and the steel oven doors were opened, the steam would billow out enveloping the wash room. The equipment was still scaling hot, yet it had to be taken out and stacked away for the next milking cycle.

Every day the local distributor, wearing a gray fedora hat and a white laboratory coat, would stop by the dairy.

"Is it all ready, lass?" he would say, more by way of a greeting than a question.

Miss Pierce would smile at him and reply, "Indeed it is. It's all ready for you." Then, loading his van with the crates of bottled milk, he drove around the countryside delivering them to his village and rural customers.

It was also the dairymaid's job to make the butter. Every Thursday, she would stand for hours churning it in a big wooden barrel that rotated off a hand held crank. When finished, she would take a portion of the butter, and using a set of hand-held wooden paddles, roll it into miniature grooved orbs. These were then stacked on a silver dish and sent over to the Manor House to be served with Lord Dunleath's afternoon High Tea. She had one afternoon and Sunday off each week.

She was in her late twenties, pretty, with honey colored hair, light green eyes, and a country girl's pink and white complexion. With her slender figure and smiling face, she could have been the fairy princess in one of my books. A delicate apparition who had stepped out of the picture, slipped off her gossamer gown, donned a starched blue dress, white apron and sensible work boots, and went to work in the dairy.

For a while after she arrived there was some speculation as to why she had not married. As the word spread that she was deeply religious, the whispering ceased. People supposed that, either her love of God was greater than her love of "a man," or more likely that her love of God had frightened off all the men.

Miss Pierce was someone that I would call "softly religious." She was never strident about her beliefs; rather they seemed to envelop her with an amorphous cloud, a condition that served to keep the earthy farm-workers at bay. The men always watched their language around her and treated her with respect.

Not long after she arrived, she organized a Wednesday night bible class at her house. It was a big treat for us; indeed any social occasion was cause for rejoicing in those pre-television days. It was especially welcome in the winter when it was dark by a quarter past four and the country evenings often seemed endless. Perhaps that is why, in those days, conversation was so important, indeed one could say that it was elevated to an art form, and an entertainment unto itself.

At Miss Pierce's house, we sat in benches placed around the walls in her Spartan, ice-cold, unfurnished spare room. It was always ice-cold in there as she never lit the fireplace and I would sometimes sit on my hands to keep them warm. There, we would each read a verse from the bible and then listen as she tried to reinforce our already extensive Church of Ireland training with her own particular interpretation of the New Testament. I'm afraid my thoughts would often wander from her bible stories and their spiritual importance. I'm not sure how she was able to discern my inattentiveness; perhaps I had some giveaway physical trait. I know I was prone to staring at the ceiling for extended periods of time when I was bored and had transported myself mentally into a more interesting scenario—usually something exciting where I was saving the day and playing the heroine.

A sharp order of, "Geraldine pay attention" was enough to snap my mind immediately back into that icy room and her biblical message.

When the hour was up she handed out sugared almonds and bookmarks for our hymnals. I collected those bookmarks and they became my private art collection. They were decorated with pictures of elegant, long-stemmed white lilies, lavender bluebells, and even modest primroses, framing gold-leaf calligraphic words of love and peace. Some had pictures of kind-faced men and mother-earth women cradled little children. On others, white sheep grazed among verdant daisy-strewn pastures while handsome robed shepherds gazed benevolently on the feeding flock.

Miss Pierce was a serious teacher who would tolerate no giggling or whispering. Any inattention was quickly corrected with a stern look and a pointed question. There was a small core of regular attendees that included my friends Hilary Reid, Ellie Chambers and Joan Foster. Joan, who lived in lived in Sand Cottage, had an older sister Margaret, who was already "religious," and who used to come until she acquired a boy friend and the need for romance then superseded the call of religion. Sometimes Lily Wilson and Elizabeth Johnson would show up, however they were already older, and it may not have seemed exciting enough for their mature tastes. Lily, I suspect, was more interested in flirting with the boys than having her soul saved, and probably attended when there were no other acceptable diversions.

Every year Miss Pierce held a party for all the bible students. It was her reward to all God's faithful children, and was magnanimously extended, not only to the regulars, but also to the prodigals that attended either sporadically or not at all. All the estate children were gathered into the fold for the glorious occasion, and were eager participants. We bobbed for apples, snapped Christmas crackers, and gorged ourselves on home-baked trifle, apple cremes, golden custards, and buttery Scottish shortbread. We played games under green and red streamers hung from the ceiling of our Spartan bible room, transformed for the occasion with sprigs of holly and a large lighted Christmas tree. That the celebration more resembled homage to Dionysus than to Jesus Christ was, luckily for us, lost on her.

The allure of bible class faded somewhat for me when, at the age of eleven, my favorite radio show "Dick Barton—Special Agent," switched its airing time to eight o'clock, which was the time we usually left our class. My friend Hilary used to laugh at the incongruity of, "Geraldine tearing out of the holy Miss Pierce's class, as though all the hounds of Hell were after her, to get up the road home to listen to Dick Barton." But this was no ordinary special agent. Here was a man with God-like powers who, each week, managed to extricate himself from the most deadly (and improbable) situations. The action was always played out against exotic backdrops, and invariably resulted in the most satisfying of solutions, with the villains either behind bars or, in some cases, deservedly dead. How could Jesus, who fought evil with kind words and forgiveness, compete with Dick Barton who stamped it out in such clever and exciting ways? However things were about to change for Miss Pierce also, and that change came in the form of one, Sam White local farmer, and bachelor with an eye for a pretty girl and a propensity for young dairy maids. Although I did not know this first hand, the word was that he had wooed every young diary maid before our own Miss Pierce had arrived. In due time, true to form, he showed up on her doorstep with, as my friend Hilary would say, "A fist full of flowers, and a sweet word for her ear." As time went by, his car could be seen more and more frequently parked on the gravel path in front of her house. It was an interesting combination, and we all chuckled over the unlikely chemistry between the religious Miss Pierce and the ladies man, Sam White. However, Miss Pierce that apparently met the one man who could edge her love of God over enough to create room for an earthly companion. Within two years she was married and living with him on his farm in Belligan.

    I don't know if Miss Pierce ever realized what an influence she was in my life, because for several years the dairy was like a home away from homes for me. I stopped by there every day to have our white enamel milk can filled with our allotment of milk. Sometimes she would let me help her with the bottling and occasionally I would operate the butter churn for her, cranking the handle until my arm ached.

    Miss Pierce was one of many important people who populated my childhood, and her kindness and guidance helped with the void created when Aunt Sally left. I remember her in so many ways, and, even to this day, any picture of a delicate flower, lambs cavorting in a field, or a kind-faced Madonna, immediately transports me back to that chilly bible-class room, my library of bookmarks, and the sweet-faced dairy maid with her comforting message of salvation.

CHAPTER SEVEN

The Farm

> *I was recently listening to a friend of mine talk about the time he had been an insurance adjuster.*
>
> *"If there was a particular place that insurance companies hated to cover," said Hank, "It was a farm."*
>
> *"A farm." I responded.*
>
> *"Yes," he replied, "Because farms have hay storage barns, and when they catch on fire, the fire is so fierce, there's no earthly way you can put it out. You just have to let it burn and then, of course, everything is destroyed."*
>
> *Hank did not elaborate, but I knew first hand just what he meant.*

One evening in November, my friend Hilary was returning home from Newtownards where she had been visiting her mother in the hospital. As the country bus was leaving the town to begin the ten mile run down the side of Strangford lough towards Lord Dunleath's estate, the eerie wail of the fire station's alarm siren suddenly pierced the misty night air. Minutes later, the big Newtownards fire engine, bell ringing, lights flashing, roared past the bus and headed down the dark, winding road in front of them.

"*Oh,*" thought Hilary, "*I wonder where the fire is.*" What Hilary did not know was that the fire was raging in the hay storage barns not a hundred yards from my home.

Our house was situated on Lord Dunleath's farm which covered the lands just outside his great walled estate. The lane, from our house down to the big iron gates that punctuated the stone estate walls, was lined on one side by the dairy and fields, and bordered on the other by grey farm buildings linked together by a succession of courtyards. The lower courtyard housed the milking sheds and the newly born calves. The farming equipment was stored in the middle yard, which also housed the big silo tower where the crops of greens were ground into silage that was used as winter feed for the cattle. In the upper courtyard just beside our house, hay and straw was packed into large barns that lined three sides of the yard. Entrance into the yard was through a long iron gate flanked on either side by a conical stone pillar.

I loved the farm, and the idea that a place without walls or furniture could feel like a home might seem strange to some people, yet that is how I felt about Lord Dunleath's farm. I was as at home in the fields as I was in my own living room. The fields around our house were subject to crop rotation and sported a new look every other year. The hay cycle was my favorite, for then the grass was allowed to grow long, and it rolled in the wind like a sea of green waves. In August, after it had been cut, it was left on the ground to dry out in the sun when it would eventually change color and morph into hay. I would tag behind the farm men as they pitched the hay strands into pointed stacks, decorating the fields with these golden cones. The conical stacks would later be encircled by a chain and dragged onto a special flat-bed trailed. The trailer was designed so that it could be lowered at an angle to the ground and slid under the hay stack. The hay stack was winced onto the trailer which was then raised and driven off by tractor to the barnyard where it was dismantled and the hay packed into the barns to be stored for winter feed.

The men would often let us ride on the trailer from the barnyard to the field and back. Although there were usually two or three tractors working at the same time, I always rode with Ted Curry, a flaxen haired ex-sailor, who had two daughters a little younger than me. He was not particularly talkative, other than to say, "Hop up on the tractor then," or to tell me what field they were working on that day. He might comment on the weather, and once he even told me that, "You'll be a right fine looking woman when you grew up." I don't know what kind of foresight he was engaging in because, at the time, I was going through my ugly pubescent stage. Still, it was comforting to be reassured that I would not always be so gangly and awkward. There was a comfortable rapport between us and I always felt protected and safe when I was with him.

All throughout the late summer afternoons, the tractors droned back and forth from the yard to the fields and back again. Of all the farm men, Ted was my favorite, and he was what was commonly known as a "good soul." Sometimes Aunt Sally stood out by our gate, waiting for us as the tractor rounded the corner by our house. She would offer us a cool drink of water, and sliced apples and berries which she had arranged on a large kitchen platter. Ted, always respectful, would touch his forehead with his right hand as a sign of respect and say, "Thanks very much, Mrs." During the school year, every afternoon when I came home, I would run down to the barnyards to find him where I would follow him about as he fixed equipment or drove the tractors about. After Aunt Sally left, I spent more time in the field and the woods, and at the seashore than I did in my own house.

On the night of the fire, daddy, who had just come home, walked into the house and announced, "The barnyards are burning." We were stunned. In a land where it rained all the time, I don't think it ever occurred to any of us that fire might be a danger. After I got over the initial shock, I remember running out of the house into the cold, dark evening and was startled to see the great line of flames and smoke lighting up the length of the barnyard. By that time, the farm manager was Jim Little, who had taken his father's place when Mr. Little senior had retired with his wife to their own farm over in Killyvolgan. I ran down to the entrance of the yard where Jim was silhouetted against the flames frantically running about waving a bucket of water; a hopeless gesture in light of the fact that the tinder-dry hay and straw had become a raging inferno.

By this time, everyone was aware of the fire, as it could be seen all across the fields. Some of my friends from nearby had either walked or ridden their bikes over to see the spectacle. For us, the fire was a big event, almost an entertainment, but for Lord Dunleath, and Jim, the Farm Manager, it was a disaster; the winter feed was being destroyed.

Also, the Newtownards fire engine had ten miles of extremely, narrow winding country roads to traverse before it arrived. So the fire was well underway by the time the engine drew up beside the yard, bell still clanging. The firemen jumped out, attached the hoses and began to spray the fire. The firemen were young and energetic but it took a considerable time to put out the fire and extinguish all the hot spots. When they were finished, the barnyard was a puddled mess, and the winter feed destroyed.

Aside from the fire, my most vivid memory from that night was, not feeling that I had witnessed a disaster, but the surprise I felt at how cheerful the firemen were. I suppose with all the emergencies they attended, perhaps some with loss of life, the destruction of hay barns might not have seemed to them to be such a tragedy. And, as a bonus, my friends were really impressed with these energetic fellows and they treated the firemen as though they were stars. After all, these lads who had saved the day, and stopped the fire from spreading to the adjoining yard, were both friendly and personable. Back in those days without the influence of television with its advertising glitz and the open communication of the Internet, to a teenaged country girl a fire man was tantamount to a conquering hero. There was a lot of laughing and banter back and forth between the parties, and the burly firemen even carried some of the girls out over the big puddles at the entrance to the barn.

"Come on lass. I'll give you a lift," one of the firemen would say, and he'd sweep some giggling girl up into his arms, ferry her out of the yard and set her down outside the gates. This astonished me because we were all used to trudging endlessly back and forth throughout the soggy winter countryside, and not one of us would have been nonplussed by having to cross a few puddles; we would either just wade through them or circle around them. In my thirteen-year-old naiveté, it took me a few minutes to realize that it was all just part of a group mild flirtation and perfectly harmless. After a while the firemen loaded all their equipment back onto the engine, clambered aboard, waved a cheery goodbye to us, and drove off into the night.

Of course, the interaction between the girls and the firemen was all just a bit of fun that brought a little levity to a serious situation, which just leads me to contemplate, as I have done so many times in my life, that, even in less than optimum circumstances, there is often a little loophole for enjoyment, should we find and choose to use it.

It was never ascertained just how the fire started, but Jim did not lose his job over it, and I expect the insurance money covered the loss, but most importantly, some country girls had a little excitement injected into their otherwise mundane lives during the great barnyard fire circa 1954.

CHAPTER EIGHT

Miss Vivienne Noble

My father was a serious gardener. Not content with just a small, staple potato patch, he planted and nurtured every vegetable that thrived in our cool northern climate. Daddy worked hard in the garden tending his carrots, lettuce, beetroot, cabbages, potatoes, peas and brussell sprouts, and in season we always had an abundance of fresh vegetables. He even had a strawberry patch and a glasshouse to grow tomatoes.

One day when my sister, Vivienne, was just four, daddy stormed into the house and confronted her.

"Vivienne, did you walk all over my carrot patch? It's flattened and the carrots are ruined."

My sister stared up at daddy towering over her and responded with an empathic, "NO, I did NOT."

My father's voice took on a warning tone as he repeated, "Vivienne, DID you TRAMPLE them?"

My sister repeated defiantly, "NO, I did NOT."

By then my father was really angry and his voice took on a steely edge. "Vivienne, I KNOW it was you."

However, instead of wilting under the pressure of my father's repeated interrogation, and undaunted by his threatening posture, my sister simply drew herself up to her full four-year-old height, glared unflinchingly at our father and indignantly declared. "I did NOT walk all over them." There was a short pause. Then she declared unapologetically,

"I did not WALK over them. I WHEELED over them."

Dumfounded, my father stared at his tiny daughter as though he could not believe his ears. My self-assured sister, focusing on the word "trampled," believed she was being wrongly accused, and that she was justified in her *protestations of innocence. She had certainly not TRAMPLED over the carrots; she had instead WHEELED over daddy's carrots—with her toy wheelbarrow. My sister, even at that early age, was able to base her denial on the disparate meaning of the two words; after all, wasn't "wheeled" an entirely different action from "trampled!"*

Daddy, whose planted carrot patch was in lumpy ruins, had probably initiated the confrontation with some type of punishment in mind. However, he was apparently able to momentarily set aside the mental picture of his annihilated carrots and acknowledge the distinction. Also, to his credit, he even managed to find the humor in the situation, and perhaps, like Lady Dunleath, he probably could not help but admire her independent thinking and determined behavior.

Instead of punishing her, he just shook his head and laughed.

I love and admire my sister; she is everything I am not, and I simply cannot imagine growing up without her. One of my first memories is of Aunt Sally telling Vivienne to take care of me on my first day of school.

"Take Geraldine's hand and bring her to her classroom," Aunt Sally instructed my sister. "And be sure to wait for her and hold her hand on the way home." So Vivienne dutifully held my hand as I trotted along the tree lined road through the estate to this strange place called school, and into Miss Bailey's Junior Infants class. I was only four and it was all new and frightening, but as long as I was with Vivienne, I felt safe. As a child, I could not quite master her three syllable name, so "Vivienne" became "Vivi," and I still use the shortened version, even though "Vivienne" is a prettier name.

Growing up, we spent a lot of time together. We had twin beds in the room upstairs in the front of the house. From our bedroom windows, we had a panoramic view of the barnyards, the dairy, grazing field, and the narrow road leading down to the tall iron gates at the entrance to the estate. When we were not at school, we read, played with cut-out paper dolls and engaged in the usual children's games. I don't remember playing much with the village-children, perhaps because Lady Dunleath did not want the village children walking through her estate, and the road around the estate made it a much longer walk from the village to our house. I think when we were young Aunt Sally kept us close to the house after school, and I think she was very protective of us. Perhaps the death of our sister Patricia had made her aware of how quickly tragic accidents can happen and she wanted to make sure we were always safe.

However, it was when Aunt Sally left that my sister's role in my life took on a new importance, for then we were left alone to our own devices as daddy was gone most of the time. In retrospect we were a perfect combination. Vivi was both independent and innovative and she liked to be in charge. I, on the other hand, reeling from Aunt Sally's loss, just wanted to bond with her and it was the need to belong that made me a good follower. The fact that I had grown so quickly and towered over her simply did not come into play. There was no doubt in either of our minds that she was the boss. When Vivi ordered, I obeyed; even when I had serious reservations about some of her schemes. My self-assured sister, however, was always ready for an adventure and absolutely *fearless*.

Like Lord and Lady Dunleath and many of the villagers, we belonged to the Church of Ireland, however many of the surrounding well-to-do farmers attended the big Presbyterian church. Their church was situated on the main street of the village and its tall spire dominated the surrounding landscape. The Presbyterian Church had a much larger congregation, and I expect there was plenty of money in their coffers. Our Sunday School was held in the church before morning services, however the Presbyterian Sunday School took place in a hall across the street the church, and it was held in the early afternoon. One day Vivi found out that their Sunday School was planning an excursion to Bangor, a resort town up the coast from us. The excursion date was just two weeks away, so lured by the promise of a fun-filled day in this glamorous town of seaside arcades, Vivi dragged me to attend the Presbyterian Sunday School classes. I was horrified.

"We can't go there," I protested. "We're Church of Ireland." (In retrospect, I protested a lot in the years we were left alone—to no avail.)

Don't be silly." Vivi snapped. "We're going."

So the following Sunday with me in reluctant tow, Vivi marched into the hall where the classes were set up in groups around a large room. She sized up the situation, approached one of the teachers and declared, "We would like to join your Sunday School. The lady looked us over and ignoring the fact that there was a significant age span between us, assigned us to the same class. Looking back, it seems strange that, since we appeared out of the blue, she never asked where we had come from, or questioned our motive.

The initial week was actually not too bad as we were just being assimilated into the Presbyterian view of the bible. The second week however, the week before the excursion, who should show up but the Reverend MacIlveen himself. It was what I feared the most—an inspection that would expose Vivi's intentions. The Reverend was making the rounds, passing from class to class, pausing to ask a question or make a comment at every stop. Eventually he worked his way around to our class. Vivi and I were sitting side by side and, as he looked the class over, his gaze stopped and settled on us. I was frozen to my seat. He had a shock of white hair and the bluest eyes I have ever seen. Those blue eyes narrowed as he inspected us.

"Do I know you two wee girls?" he asked thoughtfully in his rolling Scottish accent.

Without missing a beat, Vivi blithely replied, "Oh yes we've been here." She placed the emphasis on the "we've," as if to say, "*Of course* we've *been here, haven't you seen us!*" Of course technically, it was true; we had been there, and, even though it was only a one-time visit, for Vivi, it was reason enough to speak with confidence.

He continued to look at us, sizing us up with his piercing blue eyes. "Hmmmm," he responded as though not convinced of Vivi's sincerity, and I was sure he was reading my mind and my feelings of guilt. Then, after an eternity, during which I was sure we were going to be unceremoniously evicted, he turned on his heel and went on to the next class. Just as she had done with Daddy, Vivi stood her ground and had won the day. The following week we rode the big red double-decker bus to Bangor and spent a glorious day at the harbor, and in the shops and arcades eating ice cream and munching on sticks of candy floss.

According to Vivi's plan, we never went back to the Presbyterian Sunday school, but it was a long time before I went into the village during the hour it was in session. I was ashamed, and afraid of being recognized as one of those little opportunistic, insincere girls from that other church at the end of the village who only wanted a trip to Bangor. Vivi, on the other hand, unconcernedly went back to the village on Sunday afternoons when she felt like it, and marched past the Sunday School hall, unconcerned by what anyone might, or might not, think about her.

When she was eleven, Vivi had to have her appendix removed. After she returned home from the hospital, she announced that she had, "found her vocation." She was going to work in the medical field. It was no idle declaration, although her later desire to enter medical school with an eye to becoming a micro-biologist was doomed because of the expense involved in the education, and she settled on the nursing profession. However, for now, her first self-imposed assignment was to attempt to teach me how to make my bed with "hospital corners." Poor Vivi! I could not have cared less how the bed looked, never mind making it to hospital-approved specifications. Now if she had been teaching me how to steer a farm tractor or to harness one of the farm horses, I would have paid close attention, however in this case, she could not have had a more disinterested student.

Still, in typical Vivienne-fashion, she persevered. It didn't matter to her that she had such a reluctant pupil; my sister was determined to teach me how to fold the bottom corners of the sheet around the mattress in technically precise movements that would guarantee a compactness that even the person with the most severe restless leg syndrome could not dislodge.

"All right Geraldine," she began patiently. "You have to tuck the sheet in and then pull the top piece around level with the bed, then tuck the bottom part in and pull the top part down at an angle and tuck in very tightly."

But, I, regarding any kind of domestic task as tedious and something to avoid squirmed and protested. Ignoring my pained expression and protestations, she demonstrated how to create the perfectly tucked-in bed. "See," she said proudly, "This is what it's supposed to look like."

"What does it matter," I protested. "I never kick my sheets out anyway."

"That's not the point," countered my sister who was focused on the task at hand. "If you ever go to the hospital, they'll tell you to make your own bed as soon as you can get up."

"But I'm not ever planning on having to be in the hospital" I wasn't going to give up. I couldn't see any point in having to be so fussy with the silly sheets.

"Well just try it," she coaxed. "I'll go with you to the village, if you do." By the age of thirteen, my sister was a master of negotiation. She knew I was always ready to roam outdoors and the village was full of appealing diversions.

"All right," I grumbled. "I'll try."

I then proceeded to make multiple, fumbling attempts to arrange the sheets into the type of taut inflexible corners that would meet her standards, with Vivienne guiding and directing me all the while. Eventually I mastered it well enough to be released. True to her word, we then walked the mile to the village together, and I confess that, since then, I have always made my bed with those same tight hospital corners.

However, I think that Vivi's managerial powers really came into play a couple of years later during the summer garden fete at Lord Dunleath's estate. The fete was held to raise money for the church. On the day of the fete, the four gatehouses that punctuated the stone estate walls were opened to the villagers and nearby country folk who, for the paltry sum of sixpence, could gain entrance to the estate and the festivities. For me, the excitement of the fete was in wandering in and out of the tents. The entrances to the tents were lined with toy windmills that whirred colorfully in the breeze; and the red, white and blue bunting strung between the tents fluttered cheerfully, creating a festive atmosphere. Tea was served in the Tea Tent and there was a steady stream of people drinking tea and enjoying the finger sandwiches, jam tarts and Scottish shortbread baked for the occasion by the ladies of the church. The White Elephant tent always had lots of interesting second-hand items for sale, and although daddy usually gave us a couple of shilling to spend there, I always spent mine on decadent amount of cotton candy, and packets of fizz.

The opening ceremonies were conducted on the raised croquet lawns directly in front of the manor. Dignitaries and officials gave speeches while the locals crowded around below. That year, the guest of honor was Patricia Ford, M.P. A Member of Parliament was quite an important person, but Lord Dunleath, a member of the House of Lords at Westminster, had the prestige to lure her down to open our country event.

Two days before the fete, Reverend Jackson came out to our house. "We entered the names of all the estate children in a hat, and yours was drawn to present the bouquet to Mrs. May," he told me. "So wear your very best."

Was he joking! I had no very best to wear, and I can only imagine the collective wincing that must have occurred when the piece of paper bearing my name was read. They could not have picked a less suitable candidate for I was the quintessential tomboy without even a casual interest in dressing up or the social niceties.

True to form, Vivi took command. "You can wear my confirmation dress from last year," she directed, blithely ignoring the fact that I was already much taller than her. (It was the best dress we had between us). "And you'll have to take a bath."

We usually only took a bath on Saturday night; however this was a special occasion. On the evening before the fateful day, she filled the bathtub with hot water and ordered me to get into it. I climbed in and immediately jumped out. "It's too hot," I shrieked.

"Oh for heaven's sake," she exclaimed. Well, it was all right for her, she wasn't the one who was being scalded. Grumbling, she poured in just enough cold water to make it bearable, and dropped a bar of brown, grainy soap into the tub. She washed my hair with the same soap, and it ended up so tangled that no amount of tugging the comb through it would straighten it out.

The next day at the opening ceremonies, I was standing in the crowd behind the front row, hiding an enormous bouquet of flowers behind my back. When Rev. Jackson nodded to the crowd, it was my cue to run up the steps and present the bouquet. He nodded and I pushed my way to the front and resolutely headed up the stone stairs. All eyes were on me. What must I have looked like! I was a gangling apparition, all arms and legs sticking out of a ridiculously small white, taffeta dress, with tangled, hair flying in the breeze.

Mrs. Ford, a dream in a picture hat, and flowery, wide-skirted dress, leaned over me, probably struggling with her incredulity that anyone would have sent this pathetic creature on such an important mission, smiled and murmured, "What beautiful flowers. Thank you very much."

Unrehearsed in what my answer should be, I mumbled "That's all right," and turned on my heel and ran back down the steps, relieved to have the odious task over.

As soon as the opening ceremonies had concluded, Vivi ordered me home and out of her good dress which she then donned herself and went off in her finery to enjoy the fete, leaving me to climb back into my old clothes. I didn't care. I never cared how I looked back in those days. It wasn't until I became interested in boys that I began to agonize over my height and the way I looked. I went back to the fete and enjoyed the afternoon. I even lingered until the last tent was dismantled, as the golden sun slipped behind the stately pines, and the evening chill descended upon the trampled manicured lawns.

Our independence lasted for about two years. During that time, we had few cooked meals. The exception was when Daddy rode his motorbike up to Newtownards to buy sausages. For some reason, unknown to us, Daddy refused to set foot in the Skillen Bros. butcher shop in the village square. The Skillens were tall, beefy, red-faced men, who wore the traditional black and white butchers apron, and we can only surmise that Daddy had, at one time, had some type of row with them. Since my father was quiet and non-confrontational, I can't image how the animosity arose. As a result, on Thursday, Daddy rode his bike the twenty mile round-trip up to town to buy our meat, and we ate our Newtownards sausages every weekend.

We had few, new clothes, and Vivi and I only sporadically cleaned the house. I think that my poor father did the best he could, but he was at a loss when it came to the finer points of child rearing. And, although he was still dealing with his own loss and loneliness, he knew we needed more. So, I suppose it was just a matter of time before the inevitable happened.

One fateful day, Daddy came home and announced,

"I'm bringing a friend home to visit us tomorrow; her name is Mary."

Other than Uncle Herbert and Daddy's male friends from the motor-cycling community, we never had visitors at our house so this was a big event.

The following day, Mary rode the bus down from Belfast and we were duly introduced. She was in her thirties, short and thin, smarty dressed, and had fair hair and blue eyes. I thought she was pretty and very nice, and I was ready to be friends with this lady friend of daddy's. On the other hand, Vivi who was older and worldlier than me was more aloof and possibly suspected the real reason for her appearance in our lives. Her suspicions were confirmed at a later date when daddy announced. "I am going to marry Mary and she is going to be your stepmother."

I didn't mind as I could never have enough family. However, for the independent Vivi, it was the beginning of an uneasy, and eventually, stormy, relationship.

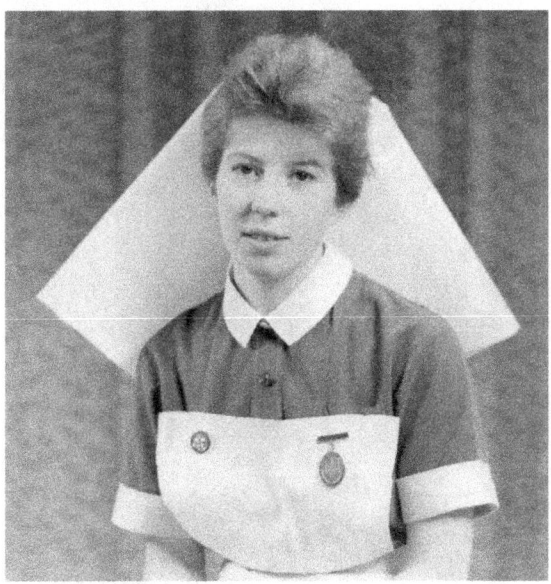

Vivi upon graduating from Nursing School

Vivi and myself on a trip home in 1978

Vivi, today

CHAPTER NINE

The Sea

> *Every summer, my family and I drive up the rugged central California coast where we spend a few days at the same quiet motel situated on a bluff overlooking the ocean. At night we sit out by the open pit fire, listen to the rhythmic roar of the waves breaking on the rocks, and marvel at the star-strewn, ink-black sky. As the evening advances, the fog bank, which hovers on the sea's horizon all day, starts to creep back towards the shore.*
>
> *Soon after, the warning moan of a distant fog horn begins to drift intermittently across the heavy sea air.*
>
> *I love this time and this place.*

At home, every Sunday we would attend services in the big grey church at the end of the village. The church was located on a low bank overlooking the sea, and was surrounded on three sides by a small, grassy graveyard sprinkled with moss-covered headstones. From the front of the church, a gravel path swept around to the vicar's house, a large white and red brick building, which was as imposing as the church itself. I always thought it strange that the minister's house, designed for one family, should be as big as the church which was required to hold an entire congregation.

We children had Sunday school classes before the regular service began. During the break between the end of our classes and the start of the service, my friends and I would sit on the low wall surrounding the church, and listen to the steady tolling of the church bell calling the villagers to service. As we talked among ourselves, I would gaze out across the Irish Sea toward Scotland hoping the mists would clear, for when the weather was good, the purple mountains on the Mull of Galloway magically materialized on the horizon, like some mystical apparition shining through the ocean haze—mysterious and beckoning.

It's easy to understand why so many of the village men went, "Down to the sea in ships." Some fished. The Dunbars and the Reagans ferried supplies out to the Skullmartin Lightship anchored on the treacherous Skullmartin Reefs, a half mile off-shore. The Macreadys and the Corrys joined the British Merchant Navy. They came home once a year sporting rare suntans and bringing exotic presents for their families. Ivan Macready even went on to be a British Bantam-Weight championship boxer. Handsome, flaxen-haired, blue-eyed Ted Curry eventually left the navy, married a village girl, had two daughters and ended up working on Lord Dunleath's farm. Shy redheaded freckle faced Bobby Curry had a tremendous crush on my fair-haired sister. When he was home on leave, he would row us around the harbor in a tiny rowing boat. We giggled and trailed our fingers over the edge of the boat through the seaweed-laced water.

"Row us around one more time," I would say over and over again, and Bobby with his eyes glued to my sister's delicate profile needed no urging to spend more time with her, even though he was too bashful to ask her to go out with him.

The sea was a way of life for us, and it gave us a feeling of permanence because it had always been there, and we knew the tides would continue to roll in and out long after we were gone. It was a part of our identity, and it provided us with that particular security when one owns a sense of place.

Since we were situated on the East Coast of Northern Ireland, we were somewhat sheltered from the big storms that roared in off the Atlantic and crashed into the West Coast. Usually, by the time they reached us most of their force had dissipated as they moved over the land. Normally our sea was fairly placid, with the waves rolling rhythmically in and out along the sandy stretches of shore on either side of the village. I loved the occasional storms that made it across the country and into our area. I would go down to the village and watch the sea thunder against the harbor wall as it whipped up fountains of spray into the air and tossed the moored boats about as though they were as light as corks. It was as though the ocean had awoken from a deep sleep and been transformed into some wildly vibrant and exciting entity.

Then, one day when I was twelve, something happened that forever tempered my romantic notions about the sea.

It was Saturday, the 31st of January, 1953. The weather was dreadful, and all day long a howling gale had swept swirling masses of ink-black clouds in from the west. By five o'clock it was dark, and my cousin, Renee, my sister, Vivienne, and I decided to go to the movies in the village. As we walked through the wooded parklands of Lord Dunleath's estate, the trees were groaning and creaking under the force of the wind. When we emerged from the estate through the lodge gates and rounded the corner towards the village lights, we could see that the normally placid ocean had been transformed into a cauldron of crashing waves and erupting spray. My sister clutched her coat about her as she strained into the wind, peered out through the darkness towards the faint winking of the Skullmartin lightship off-shore, and said, prophetically, "God help all those who are out on that sea today."

My mind immediately flashed to the words of the Sailors Hymn that we sang so often on Sundays on the big stone church at the end of the village. "Oh hear us when we cry to thee, for those in peril on the sea." This time, the prayer had fallen on deaf ears.

That morning, the big 22,000 ton car-ferry, the Princess Victoria, had set out on her scheduled four-hour run across the Irish Sea from Cairnryan, Scotland to Larne, a small sea-port, about forty miles up the coast from our village. She was one of the very first generations of car ferries, where the passengers drive their cars into the bottom of the ship over the big lowered steel water-tight doors that are afterwards closed up, fastened and then become part of the hull. At a quarter to eight, carrying 177 passengers and crew, she started out down the long sheltered inlet of Lough Ryan towards the open ocean. The sea was already rough; however the Victoria did not actually encounter the full force of the storm until she emerged into the open sea. Sailors were used to rough weather in that area, and Captain Ferguson decided to keep going. It proved to be a fateful decision, because at 9:00 o'clock a massive wave punched the big steel doors open, and the sea water started to engulf the car deck in the lower part of the ship.

At 9:45, the radio operator sent his first Morse code emergency signal.

At 10 a.m. the car deck was flooded and the ship was listing badly. The destroyer, Contest, and a salvage steamer put out from the Firth of Clyde in Scotland to find her, but their starting point was a full seventy miles away.

At 11:00 the much closer Scottish Port Patrick lifeboat also set out, and did actually reach the place from where the first emergency signal was sent, however, by that time, the Princess Victoria was sputtering, out of control, and drifting off-course, south-south-west instead of due west. The Princess Victoria did not have radar and she had essentially become invisible. The rescue vessels simply could not find her, and by this time the conditions at sea had deteriorated. The winds were gale-force winds and whipping up the sea into fifty-foot swells.

At 1:30 p.m., the Victoria was listing so badly that the Captain gave the order to "Abandon Ship." However, as the life-rafts were lowered, the fierce winds slammed them into the hull, splintering them apart, and the people on board were plunged into the frigid seas.

At 2:00 o'clock, the Donaghadee lifeboat station, situated about eight miles up the coast from our village, picked up one of her distress signals. Her position was five miles off the coast and approaching the Copeland Islands. The Donaghadee lifeboat, with her mostly volunteer crew, and four other small privately owned boats, fully aware of the awful conditions at sea, set out to try and reach her, but before they could reach her, the Princess Victoria went under. The rescue fleet spent twenty-four hours at sea looking for survivors. They picked up forty-four. But, 133 people, including every woman and child, died in the sea that had so concerned my sister that evening. At the inquiry held later on that year, it was determined that the steel doors at the car-entry point on the ferry were inadequately designed to withstand storm conditions. As result of the inquiry findings, the doors on all car-ferries were modified to ensure that this tragedy would never be repeated.

At the time, my future stepmother was still living in Belfast and working for the government. In her administrative capacity, she had received one of the mail pouches that had washed ashore. As a memento, she sent me what was left of an envelope and its contents. Although badly water-damaged, two half-lines of neat writing were still legible. It was shocking to see this letter which had probably belonged to someone who had died. This concrete evidence transformed all the newspaper headlines and the reports from the survivors into a tragic, personal, reality. For a while after the Princess Victoria sank, my fascination with the purple mountains across the sea diminished; only to re-surface one glorious summer afternoon when the sea sparkled in the brilliant sunlight, and the undulating purple mountains across the ocean formed an outline that resembled a great, sleeping, Arthurian dragon. Though I still loved the sea, I had gained a new respect for her two faces; one benign and nurturing and the other, malevolent and threatening.

However, unlike the ill-fated Princess Victoria, all sea mishaps do not have such a tragic ending, and for some they can lead to unexpected adventures.

The following autumn after the Princess Victoria went down, a Norweign freighter veered off course and went aground at the southern end of the village where, at low tide the sea retreats leaving a great stretch of sand exposed.

In the days of no television, two radio stations, and only the occasional country dance for entertainment, this was a significant event. As the listing ship swung precariously back and forth with each surge of the incoming waves, the locals gathered on the shore, shaking their head and wondering, "How that great big ship, with all the new-fangled radio equipment could have missed the Skullmartin lightship . . . didn't they read their charts . . . where was the lookout . . . . why there wasn't even a storm at the time."

This mystery fueled a lot of speculative conversation, and the events leading up to the beaching of the ship was examined from every conceivable angle for the next few days. After much discussion, the sea-wise locals eventually reached the consensus of opinion that the crew, "simply had to have their heads up their backsides at the time." According to the sea-wise locals, what other conclusion could there possibly be?

The authorities decided that the crew should be taken off the ship, and ferried to the village harbor. From there they went to the church hall where the villagers were asked to take them in, until the fate of the ship could be decided. This action created a lot of bitterness. Since the boats used to transport the crew had come from Ballyhalbert, the next coastal village three miles to the south, the residents there felt it was their right to offer the sailors their hospitality. They complained, "Just because the boat went aground in Ballywalter, doesn't mean the crew has to stay there. Wasn't it our boats that got the sailors off the ship, and don't we have the only Norwegian person to be found for miles around living here with us? Now she's going to have to travel over there every day to translate for those lads."

Controversy raged, and the Ballywalter response that, "After all it's our shore that the ships lying off, and let's keep the sailors as close to it as possible," carried no weight with the Ballyhalbertites who grumbled about it for an appropriate amount of time, then grudgingly conceded defeat.

When the crew had been taken off the ship, they were taken to our village hall where the villagers were asked to take them in. My sister, Vivienne, happened to be in the village at the time. She went over to the hall, looked the sailors over, and decided there was one to her liking, a young, handsome, redheaded giant of a fellow. She then convinced the person in charge, who just happened to be our minister, Rev. Jackson, that, "her family would be absolutely delighted to accommodate this young man for a while."

I suspect my sister didn't really care what the reaction would be when she brought him home; all that mattered was that she had her eye on him and was not about to let him get away. Furthermore, we didn't even live in the village, and she didn't have parental permission, yet Rev. Jackson released the sailor into her custody. At the time she was only fifteen, but voluptuous, attractive, sophisticated beyond her years, and ready for romance. The sailor probably could not believe his good fortune at having such a rescuer.

He did not speak a word of English, however, somehow on the mile walk home from the village they managed to establish a rapport that transcended the spoken word.

At home, we didn't know about the beaching until my sister arrived with her Viking Adonis in tow. My father was not pleased with the fact that Vivienne had taken it upon herself to foist this stranger upon us, and perhaps he was suspicious of any ulterior notion Vivi might have had in bringing him home. Nevertheless, he was gracious to the sailor and lent him a pair of his striped pajamas. We fried some eggs and potato bread for the poor fellow, who, language barrier or not, had to have felt some tension permeating the situation. However Daddy need not have worried about any clandestine romance between Vivienne and her sailor, for, much to my sister's chagrin, I stuck to them like a limpet the entire time he was there because I was fascinated by this stranger from a far-off land.

Besides, the time he was with us was mostly spent walking back and forth to the village to see when the ship would be re-floated. Eventually the owners decided to fly the crew flown back to Norway prior to the recovery operation.

He was with us for three days and by the time he left, I think all of us were sorry to see him go because he was very polite and appreciative of everything that we did for him.

When he left, he gave us the only possession he had with him. It was a big brown box camera with a peculiar odor of fish to it, and that exotic smell stayed with me, long after I had forgotten his name, and the memory of his face had faded away.

CHAPTER TEN

Aunts, Uncles, and a Stepmother

The day he married my stepmother, my father kissed me.

The service was over and we had returned to our house where my new stepmother was changing from her suit and hat into the clothes she would be wearing on their honeymoon.

I was milling around by the gate in front of our house waiting for them to leave, when, out of the corner of my eye, I saw my father coming towards me. I turned to meet him. He stopped in front of me, leaned forward, and kissed me on the cheek.

I froze. I can still vividly recall the shock I felt at the touch of his cool, slightly damp lips on my face.

He said, "Goodbye Geraldine." Then he turned and walked away. I remained rooted to the spot, stunned by this alien gesture.

It was the only time he showed me any kind of physical affection, and it has remained, forever seared into my memory, as evidence that, as far as he was able, he did love me.

One afternoon when I was ten, I had the most wondrous surprise.

It was in August, and Daddy had gone down to County Offaly on his motor bike for his customary two-week holiday. As she often did when Daddy went away in the summer, Aunt Sally had taken Vivienne and myself up the coast to stay in the nearby resort town of Donaghadee.

We were watching the Pierrot show which was set up by the harbour breakwater wall. Puppet shows were very popular back then and a staple of summer entertainment for the children. Shortly after we arrived, I saw Aunt Sally engaged in conversation with a lady over on the other side of the audience. When the show was finished, they came over, and Aunt Sally introduced us.

"This is your Aunt Violet, your mother's sister," said Aunt Sally. "She's here with your cousins, Bobby and Renee." I was flabbergasted—and delighted. More relatives! Wonderful! I could never have enough family.

Aunt Violet, a slender little lady with short brown hair and green eyes, seemed really pleased to see us.

"Vivienne," she said. "Just look how much you have grown. And Geraldine, I haven't seen you since you were a baby." She stared at me intently. "God help us!" she exclaimed. "You're the spitting image of our Cessie." Cessie was my mother's nickname.

But why did it take so long for us to find out that we had these previously unknown relatives?

Few people had telephones back then, and apparently when my mother died, my father was so distraught that, instead of telling Aunt Violet in person, he wrote a note and taped it to her front door telling her that her sister had passed away.

From then on, I think that association with my mother's family was painful for him, and only exacerbated his sense of loss. Neither he nor Aunt Sally ever mentioned them, and I think that is why we were, perhaps unintentionally, unaware of their existence.

However, Aunt Sally was pleased to see Aunt Violet at the puppet show that afternoon, and she was more than ready to chat and catch up with events.

I was in Seventh Heaven to have access to this new family. My father, to his credit, once he found out that Vivi and I had been introduced to our mother's family, was very gracious to my new-found cousins.

Renee became a frequent visitor to our country home. She never minded having to take the red, number eleven, double-decker trolley car down to the bottom of the Cregagh road where they lived, and then having to cross the busy Newtownards Road to wait for the Ballywalter bus to come by. She said she enjoyed the hour-long ride down from the city through the countryside, and the twenty minute walk to our house from the bus stop at the west side of the estate. For Renee, it was all worth it and she came to love Ballywalter and the estate. My father was pleasant to her and always gave her a bright, silver two shilling and sixpenny piece to spend in the village. I used to watch this exercise and wonder why he never gave me one.

Still, I was always happy when Renee came down, because, even though she was three years older than me, she always treated me like an equal. During our long walks along the seashore and country roads, she would tell me about the boys she liked; and then she would ask me about what was going on in my life, and then listen as though she was actually interested; a reaction that made me feel important and helped me bond with this petite, dark-haired cousin who looked uncannily like Elizabeth Taylor.

Our relationship with Aunt Violet took on a new significance after Aunt Sally left, because her house up in Belfast was a welcoming place to visit, and it introduced us to city life.

It became more important after my father married Mary.

Before meeting Aunt Violet, the only family member who visited us regularly was daddy's half-brother, Herbert. Daddy had two brothers, Sam and Vivian. (My sister was named after my Uncle Vivian). Uncle Sam joined the American Marines, fought with them during WWII, and, when the war was over, became an American citizen. Uncle Vivian joined the Royal Air Force and spent most of his career stationed in Germany.

Daddy's three half-brothers were Herbert, Sidney and Stanley. Uncle Sidney immigrated to Canada, and Uncle Stanley worked for the big Ormeau bakery in Belfast. Uncle Stanley was the colorful one of the family, and apparently lived somewhat on the wild side. Jean, my friend, Ellie's, sister was a nurse at the City Hospital in Belfast and once, when she came home for a visit, I happened to be over Ellie's house.

When there was a lull in the conversation, Jean turned to me.

"Is Stanley Noble your uncle?" she asked. Noble was not a common name so I suppose she made the connection.

"Yes," I replied.

"I took care of him the other week,' she said. "They brought him in and he was a mess. He was covered in blood and I had to cut the clothes off of him."

"Uncle Stanley!" I exclaimed. "What happened? Is he all right?"

"Well," said Jean. "He was riding his motor bike around in the Ormeau Bakery showroom and he went through one of the floor-to-ceiling plate glass windows. He was all cut up, but he's all right now."

"Why would he be doing that and how did he get the bike into the showroom?" I asked.

Jean shrugged, "I don't know, but he's lucky he didn't sever an artery."

I never saw much of Uncle Stanley, but he was a big, good-looking, rangy fellow who smiled a lot and, I suspect, was a charmer with the ladies.

The mad-cap motorcycle incident just seemed to be in keeping with his character.

Uncle Herbert was a very different person from his brother Stanley. Uncle Herbert was very smart and well read. Tall and thin and wearing horn-rimmed glasses, he looked like a college professor. I think he was very fond of Daddy because he would often come down from Belfast to our house on Sundays. Many times, they would be joined by Daddy's motor bike racing associates. Daddy was recognized throughout the racing community as an expert on all things mechanical. Riders would visit him to ask for technical advice, talk about the latest events, or just discuss strategies for winning races. They would all sit outside, and I always had the impression that Daddy was holding court and the visitors were his subjects, asking advice and paying homage. The Ireland Saturday Night newspaper once sent a reporter down to do an article on him. The article appeared in a full page spread with a picture of Daddy standing beside his bike.

Uncle Herbert was a gentle sort and Vivi and I both liked him, however, we established a different type of connection with our Aunt Violet. I suppose, as children, we accept the adults in our life without question, judgment or evaluation. People I thought quite ordinary while I was growing up, were, in retrospect, actually quite extraordinary.

Aunt Violet was one of those people. Although she was just a little slip of a thing, she possessed the strong personality that so often inhabits pint-sized people.

And, while she was opinionated, she could be flexible. She lived in Belfast, a city where profound prejudice between Protestants and Catholics had seeped into every aspect of society. Aunt Violet was deeply anti-Catholic. She abhorred the easy forgiveness of the confessional, the denial of birth-control, which led to very large, poor families, the authoritative power of the pope, and, having been brought up a Methodist, she disliked the trappings and the ornate ceremony of the Catholic religion. She was, however, magnanimous enough to have a Catholic friend from the "other side" of the city, something unheard of in the Protestant enclave where she lived.

"Molly might be Catholic," Aunt Violet would say defiantly. "But sure, she's one of the best." And I also think that, in today's more temperate climate at home, Aunt Violet would probably have softened her stance.

She loved knitting and crossword puzzles. Often when I went up there, she would be sitting by the fire, one leg curled under the other, drinking tea out of one of her many, flowered china mugs, and muttering under her breath as she pondered yet another complex word association. She was an accomplished seamstress and, without as much as a pattern to go by, she could whip up a dress in a matter of hours.

When she was seven, her mother ran off to live with another man, leaving Aunt Violet, Aunt Lily, my mother and their young brother, Tom, to be raised by their father and maternal grandmother, and I think the effects of this abandonment, and its aftermath, were subtle. I often wondered if that was why she so was obsessed with having all her clothes immaculately clean. Luckily for her, domestic washing machines had now come upon the scene. Clothes emerging from her machine were expected to be pristine. If there were any lingering smudges, or anything that looked suspiciously like a blot, the offending items were thrown back into the machine and sent through for as many cycles needed to remove all traces of dirt. I wonder if she was trying to somehow "clean" the past. Although it would scarcely be worth more than a disapproving comment today, back then, a mother leaving her children to live with another man was considered quite scandalous. And it left an unwanted stigma on the family.

She was very good to us. Her door was never locked, she was always ready to put the kettle in order to make welcoming cup of tea. I think that in some ways she was trying to make up for the lost ten years when we had no contact with them. She was not pleased to hear that Daddy was going to be married.

"Your mother would roll over in her grave if she knew your daddy was getting married again." was her initial reaction. I think she could not reconcile the fact that daddy, who had loved my mother so much and who was so devastated when she died, could actually be taking another wife, even after ten years.

I always thought that Daddy married Mary just to take care of us. Still, I think he was fond of her, and someone told me that, although Mary was in her late thirties, she had wanted to get married and have children. I expect I learned that fact from Hilary, who often seemed to know more about what was going on in our family than I did. She was my roundabout source of information. I think that, being quiet and non-confrontational, I often just blended into the furniture and nobody noticed I was there, or thought to include me in conversations or keep me informed. Besides, I spent most of my time in the fields with the farm men, or at Hilary's house.

I don't know if Aunt Violet ever met Mary, as my cousin, Renee, was the only one of my mother's family to attend the quiet wedding. She was concerned to hear that our new stepmother belonged to the austere Protestant Plymouth Brethern sect. It was what we called a "Hell Fire and Damnation" religion that did not believe in make-up, movies, women in slacks, or anything considered blatantly worldly. Although Daddy and Mary were married in our Church of Ireland church in Ballywalter, Mary soon after began to attend the village Plymouth Brethern sect; a defection that left tongues wagging and dismayed our own minister, Rev. Jackson. I don't think Daddy minded because Mary was initially low-keyed about her beliefs, and he knew her faith was important to her, especially with all the changes she was going through in her life.

But it infuriated our Aunt Violet who would sniff, "Sure a drop of lipstick and a dance on a Saturday night never sent anyone to Hell."

I don't think she liked the idea that Vivi or I might be influenced by radical religious creeds. She need not have worried. Vivi and I were far too interested in living fully to be stifled by any beliefs that might restrict our activities.

She was not the only one who viewed Mary in a less-than-favorable light.

My sister and Mary were at loggerheads almost from the beginning. My sister resented this intruder into our family, especially when Mary tried to set down rules.

In Northern Ireland, everything shut down on Sunday. It was even considered disrespectful to hang washing outside on the clothes line. After all, wasn't Sunday a day of rest? My independent sister thought this a silly rule and hung some of the clothes she had washed out anyway. This of course went down the wrong way with the religious Mary, and it was only one of the issues that sparked an ongoing contentious relationship.

When our house was redecorated, she disapproved of the rose wallpaper border Vivi had picked for her bedroom. She argued with Vivi about staying out late, when, for the previous two years, my sister had operated under her own time restraints. In short, they argued continuously, and Vivi started spending more and more time away from home with Aunt Violet—who also defiantly hung her washing out on Sundays. Aunt Violet's home became Vivi's sanctuary.

In fairness, it could not have been easy for Mary. She was used to living in the bustling city with its stores, conveniences, and easy transport. Every day she dressed up and went to her Government office job. Now she was relocated to the deep country with only the sounds of the crows in the tree tops, the lowing of cows on their ways to the milking sheds and the wind in the trees. She was used to doing all her shopping in town. In contrast, every Monday, the Ormeau Bread man would drive up to our house, open the back of his van and offer a limited selection of loaves from pull-out drawers. She had to walk a mile to the village for groceries, and once a month, the coal man would drive up to our house to deliver the coal for our fires.

He was a cheerful soul who would heave a sack of coal from the back of his lorry and stagger around the back of the house to the coal storage area. His face would be black from the coal dust and his overalls were grimy and dirty. Looking like something out of a Dickens' novel, he would come up to the front of the house when he was finished and sing out. "There's yer coal Mrs."

This must all have seemed very different from what she was used to, and when she came to live with us, she knew nobody in our area, and the only phone was the red public phone outside the village post office.

She had a sister, Madge, whom I liked very much, and who was a lot more worldly and easy-going than the restrained and serious Mary. Madge would come down from Belfast and visit us now and then, but I think that for Mary, life with us must have been somewhat lonely.

Then, one day, a few months after they were married, my friend Hilary started talking about Mary being pregnant. I looked at her startled and said, "What?"

Hilary looked at me in surprise. "Didn't you know she was pregnant? She asked.

"No," I replied. "Nobody told me."

Ten months after they were married, my little half-sister Ruth was born.

Aunt Violet and her poodle "Jane"

Daddy and my Stepmother, Mary, on their wedding day

Mary and Ruth

CHAPTER ELEVEN

Shadows

My sister now lives in a pretty village in Buckinghamshire, England.

To the front, her house borders the manicured cricket green, where, on languid summer evenings, white-uniformed cricketers play that measured, quintessential British game.

In the back of her house, my brother-in-law, David, has created a two-tiered garden designed to delight the senses. A pergola, draped with cascading vines, leads the visitor by the narrow, tree lined lawn, past tall, sculptured urns spilling over with red and pink blossoms, and into the lush, foliaged lower garden.

The garden is bird-friendly and bird-song abounds. Occasionally, a neighborhood cat will slink across the lawn stalking a feathered feast. In the afternoon breeze, the swaying tree branches create dappled patterns on the green lawn. It is soothing nature at its best.

On one of my visits home, I was sitting in Vivi's garden room looking out through her sliding glass doors at her beautiful garden. I was trying to explain why, all my life, I have struggled with depression and unhappiness.

"But just look at all you have now," said my practical sister who has spent a career nursing patients who have tangible, physical illnesses.

"I know," I replied. "That's what makes it so frustrating." I have my health, a loving husband and two great children. I shouldn't feel like this—but I do."

As I looked out into her garden, an analogy formed in my mind. I said, "It's as though, I've spent my life looking out through a glass barrier—just like these sliding doors. I can see all the good things in my life, but I can't get through the glass doors to enjoy them."

"Well, for goodness sake," exclaimed my sister. "Why don't you just get up, open the door and walk through."

"That's the problem" I replied in desperation. "They're locked, and I've never been able to open them."

In January of 1954, the big mobile X-Ray van came to Ballywalter, parked outside the Parochial Hall, and offered X-Rays as a preventive health measure. Since we had nothing better to do, my friend, Hilary, my sister and I went down to be X-Rayed. Of the three of us, only Hilary was called back to have another X-Ray; however, since many people were called back for a re-screening, Hilary thought nothing of it. If you moved at all while the picture was being taken, it was clouded and hard to read.

However, after the second X-Ray, Hilary was told to go up to the Ards Hospital in Newtownards to have another more refined picture taken. As a result of this second screening, she was told that she had a shadow on her lung and that she was to stay home from school for a month and rest. Apart from being confined, Hilary was not too worried about it as she had a cold at the time and thought that the shadow was probably because of that.

Tuberculosis was actually fairly common back then, and, before the advent of new drugs, the given cure was complete bed rest. Vivienne brought her homework back to her from Regent House, the high school we attended up in Newtownards, and we all visited her.

When the month was up, Hilary went back to the hospital for a follow-up X-Ray. The results were to be sent to Dr Briars, the country doctor who had a clinic in Ballywalter. Dr. Briars had the findings that Friday and had an appointment with Hilary on Monday.

My sister wanted all of us to go to the movies at the village theater that Saturday night, and since we knew that Dr. Briars already had the results, we went down to his house to ask if Hilary could come with us. The answer was an emphatic, "No." Hilary was to go home, and go to bed. The shadow on her lung was still there. It was the thirteenth of March 1954, and Hilary was just sixteen.

It was not until she went back to the hospital the following December for another X-Ray, that she was given a clean bill of health. The shadow on her lung had disappeared. She was given the good news on Christmas Eve, the 24th of December. She had been in bed for nine months.

When Hilary was in bed, she did not want for visitors, although her mother, Mrs. Reid, was careful that she had plenty of rest and was not above shooing out drop-ins who had stayed too long. I believe I was probably the one exception, because I went to Hilary's house every day for the full nine months. I would stop in on my way home from Regent House, as her house was on the walk home from the bus stop. I always went back later on in the day and checked to see if Mrs. Reid needed anything from the village. If she did, I would ride my bike to Ballywalter with Bunty, my Border Collie and constant companion, running along side me. After I bought the requested items, I would load them into my wicker bicycle basket, and take them back to Mrs. Reid's house. While I was inside, Bunty would wait patiently for me outside the door.

On the weekends we played endless games of monopoly, with Vivi and I sitting on either side of her bed with the board and game pieces sprawled between us.

Lady Dunleath would drop by occasionally and send over jigsaw puzzles and gifts via Kitty, her maid, who was a good friend of Mrs. Reid's and who walk over from the Manor on her evenings off. Elizabeth Johnson sent over magazines, Glamour and Woman's Own, and Reverend Jackson would stop by now and then.

"How are you feeling?" He would mumble uncomfortably. He was a kind man, but not a great conversationalist, and would stay the minimum amount of time, drop a big chocolate bar on her bed, and make a hasty retreat.

"If ever there was someone who was not cut out to be a minister," Hilary said later, "It was him. He should have been a farmer." Hilary's observation was born out by the fact that Mr. Jackson kept pigs in the back of the rectory, and seemed to be happier out in the countryside rather than in the pulpit, giving sermons, and dealing with people and church matters.

Many times when I went into her bedroom, she would be working on the small needlecraft tapestry of a scarlet-coated huntsman, riding off with the hounds; another present courtesy of Lady Dunleath.

After she had been given her medical clearance, she went to County Tyrone to stay for a few months with her Uncle Ernie and Auntie Eva. When she came back, she was offered, and accepted, the diary maid's job, as Miss Pierce had just left to be married.

I was always happy at Hilary's house, and helping her at the dairy. I was often reluctant to go home, as the battle lines had been drawn between Vivienne and Mary, and I often felt uneasy in my own home. They were like oil and water, and they seemed to disagree on everything.

I think Mary meant well, but she had been introduced into a tricky situation. She was approaching forty and was not used to children, and now she was designated as step-mother to my sister who was a strong-willed teenager, and who had been independent for the last two years. I didn't mind having her with us as I was a complacent type, and I liked having lots of family. I didn't mind if the extra family happened to be step-family.

I don't think she meant to be, but she could sometimes be insensitive. She was a very good cook, and she also baked delicious little, frosted cakes and tarts and a variety of sweets. Many evenings she and Daddy would be in our sitting room, reading in front of the fire. Around eight o'clock, she would make a pot of tea and bring in two china cups, saucers and plates, and serve them tea and whatever she had baked that day. I never felt as though I could join them and often went into the kitchen and had a piece of bread and jam. Daddy caught me doing this one evening and said, "Geraldine, I want you to come in and take something from the tray in the sitting room."

But I only did it once because I felt almost like an intruder. I might have felt differently if Mary had invited me in, but I expect she just wanted to spend some time alone with my father.

She was becoming advanced in her pregnancy, and, the night she went into labor, I remember seeing the light on in the landing from my bed as they left for the hospital. I don't even know what hospital Ruth was born in and we were never invited to go to see her. Hospital visiting hours were strictly enforced and I'm not sure if we were allowed to go in to see Ruth. I don't remember Daddy suggesting that Vivi and I visit.

Ruth was not an easy baby. She cried a lot and I have a vivid memory of Mary walking the floor after dinner every night trying to get her to go to sleep. She had a beautiful, English pram with the high wheels that raised the carriage up so you didn't have to bend over so far to pick the baby up. Vivi took Ruth over in the pram to Hilary's house so Hilary, who was still confined to bed, could see her. She held Ruth up to Hilary's bedroom window.

"She looked like a little golden fairy in her wee pale green coat and bonnet," Hilary said afterwards.

I don't know where I was that day, because I was always begging to take Ruth out for a walk, and I used to walk the countryside with her in her pram . . . that is, until one day Mary caught me running down the hill from

Mrs. Little's house, playing Speed-Racer with her and gave me a lecture about speed and danger. I never did it again.

I felt close to Ruth. It was good to have a little sister, almost a gift to replace the sister I had never known. She was beautiful. She had golden hair and blue eyes and fair skin. Mary was thrilled with her little daughter, I loved her and even Daddy stayed home now and then when Mary went out to her Plymouth Brethren meeting. I remember him sitting on a chair by the fire, smoking his pipe, reading a book in one hand, and rocking her pram with the other. She really was the golden child.

Eventually the relationship between Mary and Vivienne deteriorated to the point that they were fighting constantly. I used to leave the house with my poetry book, and, with Bunty by my side, I would go to the seashore. It was peaceful there and I loved to read my favorite poems. I was fond of Tennyson and never tired of reading The Lady of Shalot or Bliss Carmen's The Joys of the Road.

I have owned collies for the last thirteen years, and it has been my experience that they are particularly sensitive to human emotions. Bunty seemed to know that this was not the time to chase waves, but a quiet time, and she would stay by me in companion mode—my canine comfort.

Eventually, Vivi went up to Belfast permanently. She entered the City Hospital's nursing program. Although she had intended to enter the medical field, it was Vivi's way of making an early escape and maintaining her independence. Student nurses back then were required to live at the hospital in dormitories while they went through the three-year training period, and when she had time off, Vivi went to Aunt Violet's house.

Her departure left a big void, and our house was never the same after she was gone.

In August of the year after Ruth was born, Daddy went back down to the South of Ireland on his motorbike for his annual two-week holiday. Mary could not go because of Ruth, but she seemed to understand his need to escape all things domestic and spend some time in his childhood haunts. A week after he left, Jim, the farm manager, received a call from the people Daddy had been staying with. Daddy must have left the farm phone number in case there was an emergency, and it was a quick way of reaching us since none of the estate employees had phones back then. He had been taken ill, so Jim drove down to County Offaly and brought Daddy and his motor bike back.

He seemed fine to me, just a little absent minded, but he had to stay in bed and I expect Dr. Briars had come to the house to see him when I was at school. He was concerned about his tools and wanted to make sure that they had not been misplaced. When I went into his room to see him, he seemed agitated.

"Geraldine, go down to the engine house and get the big satchel, with the tools and the wires in it, and bring it back up to the house." He said, not looking at me.

"All right daddy," I replied.

When I was walking back to the house, there was an ambulance outside it. I slowed my pace, confused and afraid. It passed me on the road before I reached our house.

"They've taken your daddy up to the hospital in Belfast," Mary told me when I went into the house. "He has to have tests."

I didn't know what to say. I didn't really understand what was going on.

The tests revealed that he had a brain tumor. He was operated on by Doctor Calvert, the foremost brain surgeon in Northern Ireland. The tumor was malignant and had spread. Mary regularly went up to see him and to attend to his needs. It was not easy as she had Ruth to take care of. And since I was in school, she had to arrange for Mrs. Little to look after Ruth during these hospital visits. She had to walk to the bus stop, take the one hour bus ride up to Belfast, walk across town to get the trolley car up to the City Hospital, and do the reverse to come back home.

It was never suggested that I go up to see Daddy, however, one weekend, about six weeks after he went into the hospital, I made up my mind that I was going to go up to Belfast to visit him. Looking back, it seems strange now that no one, not even Uncle Herbert, prepared me for what I would see.

I remember walking into the small windowed ante room that led into his room. I took one step over the threshold and looked through the window. Daddy was lying in a bed that had railings on both sides. One arm was tied down to the railing and the other flailed helplessly in the air. His eyes stared blankly off into space. I stopped, frozen in my tracks. I think my mind must have shut down from the shock of seeing my energetic, restless father, reduced to a vegetative state.

I do recall turning around. My next memory is lying on a grassy bank sobbing. How I came down three floors and along a corridor to the other end of the building and out a door onto the grass, I will never know. Those five minutes, driven by shock, are gone forever.

Six weeks later, my father was dead.

I have only two memories of his funeral. One is of sitting in a back pew at the funeral home while Mary was up at the front with her relatives and Uncle Herbert, while Renee, Vivi and I seemed to go unnoticed. The second, more powerful, happened on the funeral ride to the graveyard. We were riding through the busy Belfast streets in a car behind the limousine carrying daddy's coffin, when I noticed an older man in workman's clothes standing on the sidewalk waiting to cross the street. As daddy's coffin passed by, he took off his cap, held it over his heart and bowed his head. I don't know who he was, but that sympathetic, universal gesture of respect affected me deeply. At that moment, I felt closer to that man than anyone in the funeral party. It was a momentary symbiotic relationship with a stranger.

Daddy was buried in a cemetery overlooking Belfast. From his gravesite on the hill, you could look across Belfast Lough to the hills on the North West side of the city where my mother was buried in Carmoney Graveyard. As a postscript to her statement, "Your mother would turn over in her gave if she knew your daddy was getting married again," Aunt Violet's bitter comment was, "Your mother would turn over if she knew your daddy was not being buried with her."

I don't blame Mary, but, in my whimsical mind, I wish my father and mother could have slept together—forever through the ages.

Poor Mary, she had been married for less than three years and she had already lost her husband. But the biggest blow was yet to come.

Three months after Daddy died, little Ruth—our golden child drowned.

Vivi and Gordon in Vivi and Dave's garden

CHAPTER TWELVE

Ruth

All my adult life, I have assiduously avoided funerals. I always have an excuse. I have to work, or I can't leave the children, or it would mean flying six thousand miles to get there. The truth is, I have just not been able to face such an event.

Then, the wife of the handy man where I worked died. He was such a gracious soul. I never saw him angry when people harried him to complete a task in an unreasonable time; he just smiled and said, "I'll do my best." I never heard him say a bad word about anyone, although, at times, he would certainly have been justified in doing so. He was tall and slender and his curly hair was beginning to grey a little around the temples. The Christian description would be, "He walked in grace."

I was determined to attend his wife's funeral.

On the day of the funeral, I entered the church about fifteen minutes before the service was due to begin. I sat in the rear in an aisle seat, just in case I had to slip out, because I was unsure of how I would react.

I looked around. Several large, smartly-dressed black ladies were pacing up and down the aisles carrying boxes. I watched them, wondering what they were doing, until one of the ladies suddenly wheeled around, whipped a Kleenex out of the box she was holding and handed it to a lady sitting at the front of the church. I could tell by the bent head and shaking shoulders that the recipient of the Kleenex was crying.

Then it dawned on me. Not only was it acceptable to cry at a funeral, it was expected.

It was one of those shocks that, when experienced, reverberates through the entire psyche. There was no stiff-lipped mentality here. There was only the knowledge that intense grief, when buried, never dissipates and will haunt the bereaved for the rest of their lives. At this funeral, grief was encouraged, comforted and administered to by these Kleenex wielding ladies of mercy.

It was a revelation. Without expressing grief, there can be no hope for healing.

After Daddy died, Lord Dunleath offered Mary the vacant Poultry Maid's job at the estate farm. It must have been demeaning for her to take on such a lowly job after working for the Civil Service, however it meant that she would be paid, and that we would be able to stay on in our house on the estate. In the Poultry Maid's job, she would have responsibility for the feeding of the large flocks of hens, gathering and packaging of the eggs and care of the newly-born chicks.

When she worked, Betty Little, who was Jim, the Farm Manager's wife, looked after Ruth. Betty was friendly and energetic and had two young sons of her own. Sometimes on Saturdays, or if she was not at home, I took care of Ruth.

One cold wet Saturday in February, Betty was not available to baby sit. Normally, I would have stayed with Ruth, but on this particular day I wanted to go to the village with my friends. Mary and I talked about it and she said that I could go, and that she would take Ruth with her to collect the eggs.

When my friends and I came back from the village, we were met at the estate gates at the bottom of the lane to our house by Mrs. Butler, the wife of Lord Dunleath's man servant. She was crying and out of breath.

"Oh Geraldine," she gasped. "It's terrible. It's Ruth. She fell in the pond. Mrs. Fowler came out but it was no good." Her words tumbled out, but they didn't make any sense to me, and I did not grasp what she meant. Why did Mrs. Fowler come out? She was the wife of the village Newsagent and the registered District Nurse. She was a lovely little lady with a musical Scottish accent and bright blue eyes, but what was Mrs. Fowler doing here? In my confusion, I did not connect falling into the pond with any serious consequences.

I ran up to the house to see what Mrs. Butler was talking about. Somehow in the course of the busy afternoon, Ruth had wandered off from the egg house. When Mary realized she was gone, she searched frantically for her. She found her face-down in the icy cold duck pond over by the hedges that bordered the tractor path.

They rang for Mrs. Fowler from the farm phone. Mrs. Fowler immediately drove out from the village. She tried desperately to revive Ruth. Neither CPR nor immersion in a warm bath worked. Ruth was dead.

Had I looked after her that day instead of going to the village with my friends, she would not have died. It actually took a while for this to sink in. When it did, I blamed myself. If only I had not been so selfish. If only I had stayed home and taken care of her. This guilt manifested itself in subtle ways. I began to get sick-headaches. They would come on every other Saturday, stay through Sunday, and could only be relieved when I vomited. I became more introverted. At some level, I developed the belief that I had no right to be happy. Most of all, I was angry. I was angry at Aunt Sally for leaving. If she had stayed, none of this would have happened. I was angry because my father had died, and angry because Ruth's death was yet another loss.

Because it was unacceptable to be angry, I buried it.

My stepmother was shattered. For days before and after the funeral, she stayed in bed. She sobbed endlessly, and when she was too exhausted to cry any more, the tears just seeped out of her closed eyes. Uncle Herbert and her sister, Madge, made all the funeral arrangements.

I remember walking up to Ruth's tiny white casket on the day of the funeral and looking down at her. It was another shock. I don't know what I expected as I was not asked to go up to Daddy's casket. Ruth's blond hair was neatly combed around her horribly bruised, ashen face; her blue eyes closed—forever.

Although I already had a profound sense of loss over never knowing my mother or my sister, Patricia, the finality of Daddy's and Ruth's death was overwhelming. The awareness, that I would never see or be with either of them again transmuted into a physical and emotional pain that was too deep to be relieved by tears.

Ruth was buried with my father, across the lough and the green hills from my mother's grave.

Although she was devastated by the loss, Mary found strength in her religious convictions, and I think the idea that she would one day be reunited with my father and Ruth again gave her comfort. Eventually she eased out of her grief enough to make plans for the future.

It was decided that I was going to live with her when she moved away. I do not blame Mary for wanting to leave. There were too many painful memories associated with our house and the estate. Since I did not know where else I would go, it never occurred to me to object.

But now it was my turn to be devastated. Mary had acquired another government job, however this time is would be in social services and she would be caring for a group of old age pensioners who were living in attached cottages in Rathcoole. Rathcoole was a new housing development, five miles north of Belfast City center and twenty six miles from Ballywalter.

I had to leave my beloved estate, the farm, the village, the sea shore, my friends, who were like family to me. I had to change high schools, and go to live in a place where I knew nobody.

The final blow was to have to give up my dog, Bunty.

I have to thank the gypsies for Bunty. Every summer, they used to come around in their horse drawn, painted caravans. They would camp in a grassy spot down at Three Roads End and go around to the country folk selling colored paper flowers and odds and ends. One of their dogs used to come up to our house regularly and I asked Daddy if I could keep it. Daddy, who was suspicious of the gypsies said. "No." However; not long after that, he brought home a beautiful fluffy collie puppy for me that he had purchased from one of the local farmers.

Bunty became my constant companion. She slept on my bed, ran beside my bicycle when I rode to the village, and would wait outside whatever shop I was in until I came out. She would run along the shore with me, jumping over the waves and running circles in the sand. I did not even have a leash for her. I did not need one because she never left my side.

There was no place for Bunty in among the old folk in Rathcoole. Mary gave her away to her brother-in-law who had a farm in Antrim.

By this time, I felt utterly helpless. Decisions, over which I had no control, were being made for me. As a coping mechanism, I began to bury my emotions. However, sunken emotions have a habit of resurfacing later on in life. I cannot, to this day, think about Bunty without crying. Any stray dog on the street sends a pang through my heart, and it infuriates me to hear of any type of animal abuse.

Emotional scars can eventually grow over, but I believe that they never completely heal.

The June after Daddy and Ruth died, I went to live In Rathcoole. Ironically, Carmoney Graveyard, where my mother was buried was visible from my bedroom window.

I was fourteen years old, and, had I been on an isolated desert island surrounded by thousands of miles of empty sea, I could not have felt more lonely, or isolated.

CHAPTER THIRTEEN

The Little Blue Car

Recently, during one of my phone exchanges with Hilary, we were talking about the main jewelry store in Belfast when we were growing up.

At the time of this particular conversation, Hilary, who now lives in England, happened to be home, visiting her brother, Billy, who still lives in Ballywalter.

"That reminds me," said Hilary. When I come back here in August, I'm going to take my engagement ring in to be cleaned. I still have the sales slip. It says, subject to one free cleaning."

"How long is it now since you and Walter were engaged?" I asked.

"It has been fifty years, this year," she replied. "And then we got married two years later."

"Gosh!" I exclaimed. "And you still have the sales slip."

"Oh yes," replied Hilary emphatically. "And I've never had my ring cleaned, so I'm going to take it in and show them the slip so I can get my free cleaning."

"But it has been so long, do you think they will do it for you," I asked doubtfully.

"Of course they will" she replied confidently.

There was no doubt in Hilary's mind that her ring would be accepted and cleaned—no matter how much time had passed. After all, to Hilary, a promise, written or spoken, is as good as a binding handshake.

"And why?" I said to myself, "Would she think any differently—when commitment is simply an integral part of her own character."

The next time I spoke to her, she was over in Ballywalter visiting with her brother, Billy, for a few weeks. She told me that she had indeed taken her ring in to be cleaned, and that they were very nice to her.

I asked her if they were surprised that she had waited fifty years to get her free cleaning. She laughed and said,

"No, they were more astonished that we were still together after fifty years."

So now, Hilary's ring sparkles like new again. She deserves it and I'm pleased for her.

I love happy endings

A couple of weeks after I went to live at Rathcoole, I received a reprieve. My step-mother wanted to go to Donegal with a couple of her friends for a holiday. She suggested that I send a letter to Hilary asking her if I could spend those particular two weeks with her in Ballywalter. Since the school summer-holidays had just begun, it would be some time before I started my new high school.

I wrote to Hilary who immediately responded to say, *of course you can come and stay.* Her mother, Mrs. Reid, was going up to County Tyrone for a visit, so it would be just Hilary and I in their cottage.

I loaded my wicker basket with a few things and rode the twenty six miles down to Ballywalter. It was to be the first of many bicycle rides down to Hilary's house. Later on, during the school year, I would often leave on Saturday morning, ride to Ballywalter, spend the day, have tea with Hilary and her mother, and then ride the twenty-six miles back to Rathcoole that night.

I look back now and I am amazed that I was never in an accident. I had to ride all the way across Belfast to get to the ten miles of open road leading down to Newtownards. I would then cross that bustling market town, and head down the narrow two-lane road that ran alongside Stangford Lough. Five miles later, I would turn inland at Greyabbey and ride the last five miles across the peninsula to the estate, which was situated on the seaward side.

I loved this part of the route. The road wound through pastures of peacefully grazing cows and flocks of sheep. Grey, rain-washed farm houses, wearing the cloak of timelessness, dotted the surrounding countryside. In spring, bluebells carpeted the hillside woods, and the gorse bushes, sporting their new blossoms, dotted the fields like mini bursts of yellow sunshine.

The ride back at night could be dangerous. A good portion of the way to Rathcoole was along pitch dark country roads, and I only had my small dynamo-driven bicycle light to alert motorists that I was on the road. Of course, there was not as much traffic back then, but I was still lucky to never have had a mishap.

I remember the day I rode down to Hilary's house from Rathcoole, to begin my two-week holiday with her, as though it was yesterday. I was so relieved to be going home again that I actually felt happy.

It was a mild July day. The sun was shining and the blue waters of the lough sparkled. Strangford Lough was formed by a retreating glacier at the end of the Ice Age. As the ice receded, deposits of boulder clay were left in the scoured out ten-mile section that was eventually inundated by the Irish Sea. These deposits formed little islands that dotted the length of the lough. Over the years, grass and tree seeds, probably carried by birds, had taken root, and the islands had become a verdant haven for wild life. On my ride to Ballywalter, these wooded isles, adorning the blue waters of lough, had never seemed more beautiful to me. Everything about the day felt perfect, and I did not want anything to spoil it, so I was careful to ignore the huge boulder by the side of the lough on which some religious fatalist had painted the grim prediction, **PREPARE TO MEET THY DOOM.** I had traveled up and down this road for years on the school bus. I knew exactly where the rock was, and I did not want any reminder of death to spoil this perfect day.

I had to push against a brisk southerly breeze; however I was so happy to be going home, I would have willingly ridden a hundred and twenty-six miles to get there, instead of the required, mere twenty-six. I wonder if this was the kind of day that had inspired the poet, Robert Browning, to write, "God's in the Heavens and all's right with the world."

While I was at Hilary's house, she was working in the dairy. Although I did go down to help her, I also had a lot of free time on my hands. One of the first things I did was to go to see my old house. Lord Dunleath had hired Mr. Bailey from the village to take over Daddy's job, and when we left, the Bailey's had moved into our house. When I knocked on the door, Mrs. Bailey answered and immediately invited me in.

"Geraldine, come in, come in," she said hospitably. "Let me show you around the house."

She was very gracious, and I know she meant to be kind as she knew the circumstances that led to my departure. It never occurred to me that being back in my house again might be traumatic.

The visit was a mistake.

I felt like a stranger in what I still regarded as my own home.

Our piano, on which my sister and I used to play duets, was gone. A couch had taken its place.

The familiar pictures were no longer on the walls. My favorite, The Beeches at Minnowburn," showcasing those beautiful trees with their dark trunks and glorious red foliage was not hanging over the kitchen table.

The lace curtains had disappeared from our sitting-room windows.

There was an open area where the polished, wooden sideboard that held Daddy's Napoleon Clock used to stand. Every morning before he left, Daddy would take the big key from the top drawer and wind up the clock. Now, those mellow chimes would never more mark the passing of the hours for us there.

Gone all gone!

Most of it had been discarded. I think my stepmother did not want to take memories of the house with her, and she had transferred only a few items to that strange house surrounded by the old folk's cottages in Rathcoole. She had given Daddy's motor cycles to my Uncle Jack, and, apart from our piano which did accompany us to Rathcoole, all material memories of my mother and father had been eradicated. The empty spaces, in what I still considered to be my own home, reflected the emptiness I felt at that moment. My world had been turned upside down.

I thanked Mrs. Bailey and left.

I never went back.

I never went back, but in a corner of my heart, that house is still my real home.

I returned to Hilary's cottage. At least, it was still familiar and comfortable.

That first evening I persuaded Hilary to go to the village with me. I was anxious to go to the Ardmore shop to see Walter Harris. She had never met Walter, however she had heard me talk about him, and she knew that I really liked him.

Walter Harris, his mother and his brother, Billy, had come to the village around the time Hilary was confined to her bed. They took over the Ardmore shop in the center of the main street. Hilary had gone up to County Tyrone when she was better, and then accepted the dairy maid's job as soon as she returned, so she had not spent much time in the village. She did not know Walter, and had only heard me talking about him.

I thought Walter was gorgeous and I had a crush on him. I was delighted when Hilary's mother sent me on any errand that would take me into Walter's shop. Sometimes, he was not there, and I was disappointed if I could not see him.

He was about nineteen, tall and broad shouldered with blue eyes and a great head of blond hair. And, in an era when most lads of his age walked, rode a bicycle, or took a bus to go somewhere, Walter actually owned his own car. It was a blue Austin A-50, and it would be parked outside the shop when he was working. He was always friendly to me, and if he detected my crush, he graciously showed no signs of it. I was still in an all-out tomboy stage, too tall for my age, ungainly and going through that ugly pubescent phase—not the kind of girl that attracts interest from the opposite sex.

But Walter would always engage in a bit of pleasant banter with me.

"Och, hello Geraldine," he would say. "How are you? And did you ride your bike into the village in the rain? Are you not afraid of getting wet?"

Or, if the weather was good, he might say, "Well it's a good day for a bike ride."

My favorite candy back then was "Smarties." They are essentially like the American M&Ms, and are packaged in a small brightly-colored, oblong tube. Sometimes, if I was buying Smarties, Walter would smile.

"Geraldine," he would say, feigning surprise. "Did you really eat all the Smarties you bought yesterday? Ah well, you need energy for all the bike riding you do."

And then, we would laugh together, because my ability to consume voluminous amounts of any type of chocolate was a well-known fact.

"It's a wonder you stay so slim eating that many sweets," Walter would observe. "I suppose it's because of all the bike riding. Still, you're very lucky, you know, other people would be fat if they ate as much as you do."

I think part of the reason I liked him, aside from the fact he was so good-looking, was that he was a gentle, genuinely nice person.

It was actually Billy, Walter's brother, who asked Hilary out first, but I don't think Hilary was really interested in going out with anyone at the time and she declined his invitation.

With Walter it was different; he did not give up as easily. A few days after they were introduced, he asked her to go out with him. Hilary was, at first reluctant, but Walter persisted.

"All right, Hilary eventually told him. "But we'll have to take Geraldine with us. She's staying with me and I'm not going to leave her alone."

Walter, to his credit, did not hesitate, although I'm sure he would have preferred to be alone with Hilary on their first date.

"All right," he agreed. I'll drive us all over to Bangor."

Now, you might think that, having such a crush on Walter, I would be dismayed at this turn of events. The truth is, I was delighted. I might have only been fourteen, but I realized that he was far too sophisticated for me. I was actually quite happy just to admire him and be friends. Besides, at that time, I was so shy that if a boy had touched me romantically, I would have fled the scene. No, Walter and Hilary, being together, seemed just right to me.

The two people I liked so much.

We drove to Bangor in his little blue car.

We spent that evening walking along the promenade. Bangor is situated on the north curve of the peninsula and is a popular summer tourist spot. The boardwalk, facing the Irish Sea, is lined with tall, white hotels sporting large picture-windows that provide guests with an optimum view of the harbor and the sea.

The promenade is lined with amusement arcades, and I was in seventh heaven, playing all the machines. I never really had any money of my own, but Hilary generously gave me an allowance at the beginning of the evening which I promptly used to play the slot machine games. My only winnings from the evening were two chocolate bars, which Hilary reminisced about years later.

"It would have been cheaper," she recalled in amusement, just to buy the chocolate bars." And then she laughingly added, "But then all the fun would have been lost."

Despite my presence, the date between Hilary and Walter was a success and they became an established item.

During my stay, I visited all my old haunts in the day time. At night, I would drift off to sleep listening to Pat Boone crooning, "A White Sports Coat and a Pink Carnation," or "Love Letters in the Sand," from the bedside radio. Sometimes, I was lucky enough to catch Tan Hunter singing my favorite, "Red Sails in the Sunset."

I spent time with my friends, Ellie and Joan. The weather was good for the entire visit, and it was as though some benign entity had organized everything to make my trip there a pleasant one.

I think Daddy must have felt that way when he went back to County Offaly for his two-week vacation every August. He had never wanted to leave the place where he grew up either, but he had to move to Northern Ireland with the family when my grandfather retired from the Constabulary. How he must have enjoyed being back in the town that he still considered home, visiting his old friends, and riding around the familiar country roads on his motorbike.

When it came time to go back to Rathcoole, Walter and Hilary drove me back in the blue Austin, with my bike stowed in the trunk. Although it was a glorious sunny day when I made the trip down to Hilary's house to begin my visit, the weather had now turned gloomy. The overcast sky, reflected in the grey waters of the lough, mirrored my mood. As we passed the big boulder, its message, **PREPARE TO MEET THY DOOM**, seemed chillingly prophetic. The emptiness I felt inside turned into a physical ache. Had I know at the time that I was to spend the next four years living among the old folk's cottages in Rathcoole, I would have been even more depressed.

And those years certainly did have their ups and down.

However, they were not all doom and gloom.

Hillary and Walter on their wedding day

CHAPTER FOURTEEN

Transitions

The first time I went home after immigrating to America, I stayed with my sister. Vivi had married and was living in a house overlooking Newtownards.

We were driving down into the town when Vivi turned to me and said, "You'll never believe what they've done to Regent House."

Regent House was the high school we attended. As with all high schools in those days, the curriculum was non-negotiable and strictly college-preparatory. The girls wore black, pleated tunics and the boys grey flannel trousers. Everybody wore a white shirt with a black and red striped tie and a black blazer with the red, school "fleur-de-lis" emblem sewn onto the top blazer pocket.

I believe the school itself must have once been a stately home. It was situated on bustling Regent Street near the town hall. Seeing the building façade and the interior décor, one could not help but speculate that it had once been the elegant home of some moneyed family. The rooms had heavy wooden doors, and the upper sections of the walls were adorned with borders of frieze work, that echoed the classical decorations of Greek and Roman pottery. A stained glass dome edged in eggshell blue dominated the central hall, and the upper floor was accessed by a graceful, sweeping split-staircase.

"What has happened Regent House?" I asked Vivi, surmising from her disapproving tone that whatever change had been made, it was not for the better."

"It's a car wash!" she exclaimed. "Can you believe it? Regent House is a car wash."

I was stunned. That beautiful building, that place of higher learning, now a commercial car wash!

As we drove by, I stared in dismay at the cars lined up in the front of the old Regent House, waiting their turn to be washed.

"But, where's the school now?" I asked.

"Oh, they built a new, modern one, with playing fields, over on the north side," she replied. "Apparently it's a lot bigger and really nice."

Well, I couldn't argue with the rational of creating a larger, more contemporary school, but I hated what had happened to my old alma mater.

"They could have at least done something more appropriate with the building." I said. "They should have made it into a museum, or even an art gallery."

My sister thought for a moment and then sighed. "Sooner or later," she replied stoically. "Sooner or later everything changes and we just have to go with the flow . . . .

I have always loved school. Whether it was standing around the blackboard in Miss Bailey's Junior Infants class reciting the multiplication tables, or working towards my graduation from college at the age of sixty-three, school has always been one of my happiest experiences.

My first school, Ballywalter Primary, was situated on a rise above the village square. It was accessed by a curving series of steps that were bordered on either side by cheerful carpets of orange and crimson nasturtiums. I loved those flowers with their cheerful faces and trailing vines. I always felt as though they were welcoming me, as I made my way up to the classrooms.

The school was bordered on two sides by fields, and there was a grassy expanse that ran the length of the building where we would play at lunchtime. From the square at the entrance to the school, one could look across the village street to the Irish Sea. Often, off in the distance, we could see the merchant ships that traveled up and down that much-used shipping corridor. It was a timeless setting that became imprinted on my young, romantic mind. Even back then, at such an early age, I loved and appreciated my bucolic environment.

Every day, I looked forward to school, and the lessons learned there have stayed with me all my life. In Miss Bailey's Junior Infants class, we would stand in a semi-circle around the blackboard and recite, in sing-song fashion, our addition, multiplication, subtraction and division tables over, and over, and over, again. If a student would stumble on an answer, he or she would be carried along by the chorus and quickly regain his or her footing. To this day, I can do simple computations without thinking, because I "see" the answer. This is not because of any mathematical prowess on my part; it is simply because the end results are so embedded in my mind—thanks to those endless sessions around the blackboard. I also think that, because we sang the answers, and because it did not seem like actual work, our enjoyment of it actually strengthened the retention process.

It was in Mr. Powell's class that I learned about our Solar System and the Universe. Since "Journey into Space" was my favorite radio program, I found this information fascinating. Could Mars really be inhabitable? Which place, out there in the inky blackness could my radio, space travelers be going? Living in the deep country as we did, on moonless nights, the countryside was pitch-dark, and the heavens were sprinkled with twinkling stars.

My favorite constellation was Orion. Thanks to Mr. Powell, I was able to identify him as the celestial hunter who traveled with his dog, the constellation, Canis Major. Always ready to retreat into whimsy, I saw him, not as a savage hunter, but rather as a gentleman conqueror, who, with his sparkling belt and glittering sword, ruled his star-strewn domain. I loved the night sky and was often inspired to write poetry.

> Where is there peace but in the silence of the night
> A shooting star trails out of sight
> Against the velvet midnight of the sky,
> And I am as sad as the night wind's sigh.

These might just be childish ruminations; however anyone who has spent evenings in a darkened rural environment will know that the sheer beauty of the night sky can evoke the most profound human emotions.

Years later, after marrying my astronomer husband, my romantic notions of the sky changed.

"It's actually really ugly out there," was his response to my rather naïve rambling about the mysterious and beautiful heavens. His dissertations about "exploding galaxies, black holes, and rogue asteroids that could be headed for earth any day," effectively ended my romantic involvement with the stars. All my poetic, celestial fantasies were swept away when confronted by the cold, practical face of realism. However, I'm still grateful to Mr. Powell for his enthusiasm, his colorful lectures, and for sparking a kindred response in me.

The last two years at Ballywalter Primary were taught by Mr. Lindsey, the headmaster. The two classes were held in the same room, with the lower division class on one side and the upper division on the other side. Mr. Lindsey task was to prepare us for the high school entrance exams. This fairly extensive testing was held up in Newtownards, and it lasted approximately half a day. The results of our entrance exam determined our high school category. The placement was the same as the college grading in America. The "A" group had the "very smart" classification. The "B" group was "above average." The "C" group was deemed "average."

Based on the exam results, I was placed in the "A" category. I was to be in the "Lower Three A" form. The following year, I would be in "Upper Three "A" form. The next year, I would be in "Lower Four A" form. The year after, I would be in the "Upper Four A" form. The last two years were the Fifth and Sixth Form. The class that the student was assigned to stayed together for the entire six years of high school, and the students would travel together from one classroom to take whatever subjects were assigned to each day's schedule.

I hated the Lower 3 "A" class; it was populated by the brainy students who were academically driven. I felt out of place with these serious and humorless classmates. I was desperately unhappy during my year with that highly intelligent, solemn "A" class.

My grades plummeted, and the following year, I was redirected to the "above average" Upper Three "B" class. This was more like it! These boys and girls were funny, talkative, and friendly. Having these characteristics did not seem to detract them from getting the schoolwork done; even though the curriculum was quite rigid. Latin, French, English, Geography, History, Math, Science, Art, with Domestic Science for the girls and Woodwork for the boys. The "B" group was a much better fit for me, and it was not long before I had acquired a new best friend—Marianne Roundtree. We became chummy with some of the boys in the class. Desmond Gray, Lindsey McCartney, Tom Robinson, Marianne and I always sat together class.

I actually fell in love with Desmond Gray. Dessy had yellow hair, ocean-blue eyes, charm, and a sense of humor. He was, unfortunately, shorter than me, and, although I knew he liked me, he certainly did not want a girlfriend who towered over him. No. Dessy romantic ideal was the dark haired, pixie-faced, sapphire-eyed Marianne, my best friend. I watched Dessy's crush on Marianne grow, resigned to the fact that no boy would ever find me romantically attractive. However, although he was smitten with her, Marianne was only interested in Dessy as a friend. I wonder if the college and career bound Marianne had a premonition about the easy going Dessy. I obviously shared none of her insights, for I was astounded to hear, years later, that he had joined the Royal Air Force right out of high school, gone to England, married an English girl and had four children in quick succession. I tried to imagine the charismatic and quick-witted Dessy living in a military-issue cracker box of a house bursting with children. At first it seemed like an incongruous scenario, however he was in the R.O.T.C in high school, so he was really fulfilling his wish, and with his great sense of humor, I'm sure he made a success of his life.

Marianne was an even mix of seriousness and light-heartedness. She was very clever and was probably in the "B" group for the same reason as myself. Her love of fun and intrinsic high spirits kept her from being a book-worm. Her father owned the Pub on Regent Street, just across from the school. It was a lucrative business, and it was obvious, by her house with its heavy polished furniture, thick carpets and room ornaments, that the family was quite well off. Her father was a heavy, red-faced affable man who was always very nice to me, and I was even invited to go with them on a Sunday family outing.

We drove down to Analong, which was further down the coast, and Marianne and I beach-combed while the adults sat at a picnic table, chatted and watched the waves. On the way back, we stopped to eat in the dining room of a large hotel. I ordered sausages and beans, and half way through the meal, I was struck with horror. What if I had to pay for myself? I didn't have any money. We didn't get pocket money and if I wanted to buy something, I had to ask Daddy for the specific amount. I was in an agony of suspense throughout the rest of the meal, even refusing desert, due to my lack of funds. When the bill came, it was on one check that Mr. Roundtree took from the waiter and paid. What a relief, for, although I was fourteen, I was not used to eating out at fancy places, and it was an interesting lesson in family invitation etiquette.

After Daddy and Ruth died, I had to leave Regent House as Rathcoole was on the other side of Belfast and it was too far to have to take the two buses required to make the journey back and forth. Having to say goodbye to my friends at Regent House was very painful. We had been together all day, every day throughout the previous two school years, and they were in some sense like an extended family.

On my last day, the class gave me a book by my favorite author at the time, Neville Shute. The book was, "Landfall." It was about a pilot during World War II, and the class had written individual inscriptions inside the cover. They all talked about how much they would miss me. Little Nanette with the thick, wavy fair hair gave me a tiny album with a few pictures that she had taken of the class around the playground. I believe these actions might be fairly common in schools today. However, back then when life was more Spartan, it was really extraordinary that someone had orchestrated such a touching farewell. I was so overwhelmed that I could only mumble, "thank you," because I was afraid that, if I said any more, I would begin to cry.

Since we had moved to Rathcoole a week before the school term was over; it was decided that I would just travel from Rathcoole to Regent House to finish out the school year. I still have a vivid memory of leaving the school grounds on the first day I went back to Rathcoole. I did not go down Regent Street, with my friends, to catch the green number ten bus to Ballywalter, as I had done every day for three years. I walked directly across the street by myself to get the bus that went the opposite way—up to Belfast.

As I waited for the bus, the physical pain began. I should have been going home, down the road that ran alongside the blue lough. I should have been getting off at the corner by the groom's house. I should be walking down past Ellie's house, past Hilary's cottage, and up the lane to my own home. Instead, I was going to an empty house in an alien place, surrounded by the old folks' cottages, where I knew nobody. The pain intensified and became so ingrained that just thinking about that day resurrects it in all its intensity. It was one of the low points of my life.

It was six weeks before I had to start my new high school where, again, I knew no one. I would have just turned fifteen when I started there. It's an age when young people desperately want to belong, and I felt as though I did not belong anywhere.

I could not have known at that point, that Ballyclare High, my new school, would welcome me with open arms, and that I would come to like almost as much as Regent House.

I suppose high schools reflect the personality of their headmasters. Our principle at Regent House was a Mr. MacDonald, who just happened to be an ex-army officer. He was a rigid disciplinarian and I expect the way he ran the school was probably just an off-shoot of his own military training.

However, not all of the teachers there reflected his philosophies, and we were lucky enough to have an eclectic range of instructors. At one end of the spectrum was our beautiful, long-legged, dark-haired French teacher,

Miss. Jones. We all loved her because of her pleasant manner, and I think one could probably factor in a tinge of lust where the teenaged boys in our class were concerned.

At the other end of the spectrum resided our Latin teacher, Mr. Bateman. I only ever saw him smile once, and I think he was absolutely devoid of any sense of humor. He had a long pointed face, and he reminded me of the rolled up dry parchment that the Roman scribes toiled over as they recorded their deeds and documents. I dreaded the days when we would walk into class and he would say in his monotone voice,

"Take out your Caesars Gallic Wars."

Reading about Caesar's campaign records, in ancient Latin, was like trying to wade through treacle. I think we all hated Latin, and after class, invariably, one of us would recite our favorite verse.

> Latin is a language,
> As dead as it can be.
> It killed the ancient Romans.
> And now, it's killing me.

My sister recently confessed that she and her friend, Moira Cassells spent a good portion of their Latin classes drawing dolls and doodling and completely tuning him out. Fortunately for her, my sister is very smart. She would whip through her homework, or not even bother to do it, while I toiled conscientiously every night over all my reading and math assignments. Vivi's lack of dedication to her school studies never seemed to hurt her grades. Like many highly intelligent people, I think she viewed school as a bit of a bore. It was an attitude that completely changed when she entered the nursing field and pursued her true vocation.

Unlike the tall, ramrod-straight Mr. MacDonald, the headmaster at Regent House, the principle at Ballyclare High was a little man with a pleasant disposition. His humanistic approach to life seemed to communicate itself throughout the school. The curriculum was identical, however the classroom atmosphere was much more relaxed. Later, when I left to join the job market, the reference he wrote for me held words and phrases like "highest caliber," "excellence," "give of her best." I can only surmise that he concentrated on the grades that set me at the top of my class in English, French, History and Geography, and pointedly ignored the fact I that I just scraped through on all the Math and Science classes. Considering that I was going to do office work, and that excelling in Math would have been the optimum good grades to have, I think it must have been his philosophy to give all those students who did not go on to college the best possible assist as they entered the work world.

I made friends at Ballyclare High. Valerie and Rita took me under their wing and I was able to have the kind of camaraderie with them that I craved. I also acquired a boyfriend. Martin Caldwell was in my class and because of a long illness he had missed a school year, so he was older than me. He had obviously fully recovered because he played rugby for the school's First Eleven Rugby Team, and he would often show up on Saturday night banged up and bruised from his afternoon game. Our dates consisted of long walks, or occasionally we would go to the movies. For all that he was tall, broad-shouldered and athletic; he was a gentle soul, and quite shy. We went out for weeks before he actually kissed me and our physical romance never progressed much beyond that.

I broke off with him after about six months, and, until I left Ballyclare High, he constantly tried to get back together with me again. I look back and realize that I left him, because I did not want to be that close to anyone again. I had internalized the idea that being close to, and loving someone, meant eventual loss and pain. It was a strange dichotomy because by that time, I had come to believe that, the only place one found love was in romantic relationships. However, when I became involved with someone romantically, I inevitably retreated when the romance threatened to become serious. It was not until years later, with the birth of my first daughter, Kathleen, that I was able to give unconditional love and feel profoundly connected with another human being.

Poor Martin! He never gave up and it was a long time before he went out with another girl. By that time, I had already left school and had joined the work force. But I never forgot him for his integrity and for the true gentleman he was, and I retain a deep affection for both my high schools, and the friends there that helped alleviate my loneliness.

CHAPTER FIFTEEN

The Dances

When I was eleven, I decided that I wanted to become a ballet dancer. On the evening I was enthusiastically relayed this information to my father, he happened to be sitting at the dining room table. He looked up from one of the electrical schematics he was always drawing, and stared at me. After a moment, a smile began to play around his lips.

He said, "Well Geraldine, if you do, they're going to need a reinforced iron stage to hold you." Then, he laughed.

I was crushed.

Now in Daddy's defense, I have to say that this conversation took place in 1952, in an era long before the psychological profession began touting the importance of promoting a child's self esteem. Back then, nurturing children meant feeding them a "nice piece of fish" and a "big boiled potato" that had been freshly dug from the garden. Daddy certainly never meant to be cruel. However, since I was well into the ungainly phase, too tall for my age and endlessly clumsy, I imagine the mental picture of some characteristically small, slender male ballet dancer trying to heave me up onto his shoulder, and whisk me around the stage, was just too ludicrous not to elicit some type of humorous response.

But, in some small corner of my psyche, the idea that I would always be too tall and clumsy to ever be a proficient dancer settled—and remained.

Forty-five years later, my husband and I took up ballroom dancing. It is a highly technical discipline that requires excellent coordination and cohesive compatibility between partners. We are currently silver-level dancers, and I *have danced in four different ladies synchronized showcase performances. All the showcase dances are choreographed and require precision movements.*

I have often thought, "If only Daddy could be here to watch me gliding around the dance floor in my silver shoes and elegant gown."

Afterwards, I would have given him a big hug and said,

"Look daddy. I can dance after all."

I like to believe that as he watched, he would have been proud of me, and also relieved to find that his ugly duckling daughter had eventually managed to transform herself into a dancing swan.

The only dance experience I had, before my decision to become a ballet dancer, was a short-lived stint at a dance class at Ballywalter Parochial Hall. My father, doubtless in pursuit of our cultural development, had enrolled my sister, Vivienne, and myself in a session for nine to twelve year-olds. My only memory of the ill-fated class is one of dancing around the room holding my skirt out to the side with one hand, while watering non-existent flowers with an imaginary watering can. All this was performed to a simple tune that the teacher played on the piano while calling out, "Skip higher girls," or "I want nice straight backs." Alas, all I gained from this experience was a reputation for clumsiness.

The fact that I was so tall also played against me, both physically and psychologically. I became very self-conscious about my height. It didn't help that my sister and my cousin were so petite, and that I towered over both of them. Compounding my uneasiness was the attitude of some of the villagers who, every now and then, would come up to me and exclaim in disbelief, in a way that only the Irish have.-

"God help us, are you *ever* going to stop growing? What are they feeding you at home? How tall are you now anyway?"

How I ever thought I would make a ballerina just shows how much of a dreamer I was, and for a while I did cling to the fantasy.

My first real dance was in the little resort village of Millisle, just up the coast from us. It was a boisterous affair attended by the locals and many of the city folk who came down to spend summer weekends in the crème-colored caravans parked along the dunes at the southern end of the village.

I was wearing a blue and white dress my Aunt Violet had made for me, and in the fashion of the day it had a long, full skirt and lots of petticoats.

At the dance, all the girls were lined up on one side of the floor, and all the fellows were on the opposite side. But as I looked over that great divide at all the male population, I realized that, if I looked straight across, my line of vision took me over the heads of most of the lads milling around, who were, in turn, sizing up all the girls beside me.

Now, since I was a good head above the petite, cute girls on my side, I realized that I'd have to something quickly if I didn't want to end up a wallflower; the *worst possible* scenario for an insecure fifteen-year old. So I instinctively, slowly began to slump down on one leg. What I was doing wasn't obvious under my long skirt and it took a good *three inches* off my height.

The band that night was comprised of the traditional mix of accordions, fiddles, drums and flutes, and the members executed the jigs and reels with skillful abandon. Indeed, it was hard to tell who was having the more fun, the dancers, or the musicians themselves.

And then, I saw *him* heading across the floor—straight towards me. I knew this was someone special—because he was wearing a white shirt. A white shirt at a country dance! This was obviously a fellow of some importance, down from the city for a holiday weekend. As it turned out he was a student at Queens University in Belfast at a time when only the elite attended university. And, what a gentleman he was. He didn't even flinch when he realized that his eyes were on the same level as my nose.

Now, if I'd had any sense, I would have learned at least a few of the intricate steps that comprise the country dances before I actually went to the dance. But, I was naïve. My optimistic self told me, ahead of the dance, that all I had to do was to prance around the room to the music.

It was a bad decision on my part.

Panicking at the last moment, I did have the presence of mind to mumble as he led me onto the dance floor,

"I'm afraid I'm not very good at this one."

Translation—*I don't have a clue as how to do this dance.*

But he responded politely,

"Don't worry, I'll just guide you through it."

Well, it doesn't quite work that way as the band happened to be playing The Gay Gordons, and anyone in their right mind would have balked at the idea of performing those twisting, turning moves with a novice. However, something about me must have appealed to him enough to say, "It's all right. I'll show you as we go along."

Well, the dance was a disaster.

I alternately kicked his shins, trampled his feet, and almost dislocated his shoulder as I turned the wrong way. But he was such an incredibly good sport about it, and even with all the lovely, *little* girls that were there, he kept coming back and asking me to dance. I somehow stumbled through the rest of the night, embarrassed at my ineptness, although becoming a little more adept as the evening wore on.

However, I have to wonder, in hindsight, if he was some sort of closet masochist. If so, I certainly fulfilled his need for pain. He had to have been black and blue the next day. And, why else would he have continually asked me to dance when there were so many pretty, *little* girls there that night?

Although he was a student at Queens University, I'm afraid his learning must have stopped at the intellectual level, for it certainly didn't include good sense or survival skills. I can only imagine that he must have gone home and soaked his poor feet in a basin of warm water and Epsom's Salts. Still, by choosing me repeatedly out of the overflow of women there, he gave my shaky self-esteem an inestimable boost, and I've never forgotten his patience and tenacity, even though I have long since forgotten his name.

Later on, after my stepmother and I had moved up from the country, I discovered that one of the redeeming features of living on the outskirts of Belfast was the nearby availability of the Saturday night dances. The various city dances offered an eclectic musical mix. I often went on Saturday night to Queens University, however I preferred the dances at the Belfast Tech., where there was sure to be a Dixieland Jazz band playing all the Humphrey Littleton releases. The shop girls and waitresses favored the Fiesta, a slightly gaudy dance parlor where the Teddy Boys, in their Edwardian suits and slicked-back hair, nudged each other as they eyed that night's crop of girls, or "talent" as they were admiringly called.

In the summer months, the Floral Hall, up on Cave Hill overlooking the city, opened for the season. There, dancers could whirl around the polished floor under revolving spheres of pastel lights, or sip soft drinks while they watched the lights of the night ferry as it slipped down Belfast Lough, on the way across to England.

The dances I attended at Queens University and Belfast Tech. required none of the fancy footwork of the traditional dances. At Queens, the floor was often so crowded that the only requisite was a simple box step, or the basic swing movements to the jazz numbers.

During the Saturday afternoon pre-dance ritual, I would take the bus to my Aunt Violet's house at the top of the Cregagh road in Belfast. Aunt Violet always hung her key on a cord so that it would dangle on the inside of the front door, down past the slot where the postman dropped her letters. That way if any of her extended family would decide to visit when she wasn't there, we could let ourselves in to wait. She liked to go shopping on Saturday and, since I usually got there first, I would go in, tidy up the place and put the kettle on for tea. My aunt would arrive laden with purchases that she would unceremoniously dump in the kitchen before sinking into a chair saying,

"I'm desperate for a good cup of tea, and I have to sit down for five minutes and take the weight of these feet for they're killing me." It wasn't surprising. Aunt Violet was about an inch shy of five feet, and she wore heels high enough to keep any normal person's back perpetually out of alignment.

We would sit around in the afternoon talking, and then in the evening my cousin Renee, and my sister and I would go off to the dance at Queens University. How I envied them. Cousin Renee, looking like a miniature Elizabeth Taylor, and my sister, Vivi, poured into a sleek red velvet dress, teetering around in matching stilt high heels. Beside them I looked like an awkward giant, all gangling arms and legs looking incongruous in a taffeta skirt and flat shoes.

Still, someone always asked me to dance.

Since the dress code at the time called for voluminous skirts with multiple petticoats designed to create a wide swing as one twirled around, I spent numerous lunch hours in C & A's department shop on Royal Avenue going through pastel colored net petticoats checking for their swinging potential. Of course, the effect was somewhat diminished since I was regulated to flat ballerina slippers. I developed the habit of standing with my back straight, but with one knee bent under my skirt. It created the illusion that I was quite a bit shorter. When someone asked me to dance and I straightened up to walk over to the floor, it was too late, and at that point good taste would never have permitted him to bow out. Although this deception pricked my conscience, my despair over my height always prevailed, and the slumped stance became a staple decoy during my dancing days.

The Floral Hall was the place to go in the summer when the Universities were closed, and the students gone home for summer holidays. It was a popular spot for dancing, meeting members of the opposite sex, and just talking. In those days, the dances were the place to go to initiate a romantic relationship. It was a safe, vibrant atmosphere and, should a couple "click," there were safety parameters in place to protect the woman. It was perfectly acceptable for a girl to allow a potential suitor to escort her home.

Transportation in Belfast at the time was provided through a network of electric trolley cars that connected the City Proper to all of its suburbs. The red double-decker trolleys ran from six a.m. until midnight, allowing the prospective suitor to escort the chosen girl home, and then catch a connecting car to his own residence.

The Floral Hall was an elegant place, worthy of my best white linen dress and matching orchid earrings, and it was frequented by a much more sophisticated crowd than the one that attended the school dances. Some of the men who went there actually owned cars, a dubious distinction in my opinion, and one upheld by my sister who occasionally had to ward off unwanted romantic advances when she accepted rides home. I always felt a little out of place at the Floral Hall, and was more comfortable dancing in the University gymnasium with poor students who could only offer to accompany a girl to her door via the non-threatening environment of a city bus.

Tom was the one exception.

He was tall, handsome, broad-shouldered and slim-hipped, and he was the leader of the resident jazz band at the Tech. He played the trumpet and I thought him very dashing, though I admired him from the confines of the dance floor where pretty girls were the rule rather than the exception. Often during the intermission, when twenty minutes of records gave the band a respite, the members would take to the floor and dance with various girls. Why Tom picked me out of the crowd one Saturday night, other than I stood a head above all the other girls and was clearly visible, I still cannot fathom, yet for two weekends in a row I was his chosen partner. On the second Saturday night he asked if he could drive me home. Flattered by his offer, I quickly agreed; however, when I told an acquaintance she looked at me askance.

"He has a terrible reputation," she said ominously. "You'll be wrestling with him all evening." Well, even back in that tender age, I was a trusting soul who always believed the best of people, and tended to discount any bad press until it was proven otherwise. Besides, I was beguiled by the attention of such a romantic and, to my mind, important character.

When we left the dance and I saw his car—a convertible roadster—my Aunt Violet's words leaped to mind.

"It's always a fast car for a fast fellow." So, on the way home prompted by some emerging survival instinct, I blurted out what my friend had said about him.

"Indeed?" was Tom's only comment after a short silence. He then went on to talk about music, school, and generally kept up the conversation for the remainder of the ride.

When we arrived at the house, he came around to my side, helped me out, walked me to the door, planted a brief, innocuous kiss on my lips, and wished me goodnight. *Well,* I thought to myself afterwards. *He behaved like a perfect gentleman.* Still, my intuition whispered that my spontaneous accusation had sparked some streak of chivalrous pride, and without my fearful admonition the evening could have turned out quite differently. He never offered to take me home again, and I was happy to leave it at that.

From then on, it was back to the safety of the city busses, respectable escorts, and the awakening realization that trust needs to be tempered with a healthy dash of caution.

Generally speaking, though, the dances simply offered a good time. For a large segment of the youthful population, the lilt of music, the laughter, camaraderie, and the sheer of joy of the physical exertion, warmed many a dreary winter weekend. For myself, from that first auspicious occasion in Millisle, and then on to Queen's University, and the Floral Hall, those dances filled a creative and social void in my life and, to this day, they remain a happy and often revisited memory.

Myself and Gordon Dancing at D & D's
showcase in December 2007

Myself and Gordon Dancing at D & D's
showcase in December 2007

CHAPTER SIXTEEN

Belfast

A few years ago when my cousin, Margaret, came over to visit, she brought me a beautiful, golden-framed picture of Belfast City Hall. As I looked at the picture, the memories came flooding back.

Between the time I left Ballyclare High and immigrated to America, I worked in the accounting office at R.E. Hamilton & Co. Ltd; the main Ford dealers for Northern Ireland. Their sales office and repair garage was located on Linen Hall Street, directly behind the City Hall.

The City Hall, with its Victorian architecture, soaring domes and intricate design, is set in an acre of manicured lawns, and surrounded by a circular street that accommodates the rotating city traffic. Back then, the street was punctuated with various bus-stops where prospective passengers could catch one of the red, electric trolley-cars that would quietly whiz them to their suburban destinations.

It was an opportune location for all the office workers inhabiting the nearby businesses. On warm summer days, we would congregate on the lawns around that beautiful, domed building and eat lunch on one of the park benches. Then, if we were so inclined, we could just lie on the grass and close our eyes while soaking up the welcome sun. On certain days of the week, a military band, smartly dressed in gold-braided uniforms, would assemble on the nearby bandstand and entertain us with rousing Sousa marches and light classical music.

And, if after lunch, we needed to bring a little of the outdoors back into the office, we could purchase an inexpensive bouquet from one of the flower-sellers that frequented the entrance to the City Hall grounds. I was *fascinated by these ladies. They were always there, rain or shine, and in cold weather they would sit wrapped up in shawls, and wearing gloves with the fingers cut out; an improvisation that allowed them to more easily pick out the individual stems from the large buckets that housed all their flowers.*

In winter when the damp, grey pavement reflected the gloomy overcast skies, the kaleidoscope of red, blue, lavender, pink and yellow blossoms reminded winter-weary passersby of pleasant summer days. And, perhaps it was being surrounded by their fragrant and colorful wares that helped to keep the flower seller's spirits high.

"Here you are dearie," each flower seller would say to her customer as she handed over the purchased bunch of flowers. I used to marvel at how they all managed to maintain such a cheerful disposition, even on very cold days after they had been sitting outside from early morning until late afternoon. It must have been a hard life, but they certainly added color and character to the City Hall grounds.

On the days when I had a little extra money, I would eat lunch at the Chalet D'Or; a restaurant situated in a glass-covered arcade of high-fashion shops, just off the city center. There, amid tall potted palms and the clink of fine china, I could order finger sandwiches and tea, and listen to a mixture of current show-tunes being played by an older lady in an out-of-fashion dress and a feathered hat. I always had the feeling that she had seen better times, but was now reduced to playing lunch-time piano in order to supplement some other meager income.

I have to admit that, after growing up in the country, I did not care for the noise and bustle of city life. However, living on the outskirts of Belfast allowed me to spend more time at my Aunt Violet's house, even though we lived on opposite sides of the city. Her home became my refuge, and, being able to visit her helped as my loneliness intensified.

In the months after we moved to Belfast, Aunt Violet's house gradually became an oasis away from my increasingly religious stepmother. The brightness and warmth of Aunt Violet's home was in stark contrast to the gloomy atmosphere of the lonely Rathcoole house and the old folk's cottages that surrounded it.

At Aunt Violet's, the kettle was always on the stove, poised to produce a quick cup of tea for anyone who happened by. The red geraniums on the window-sill would emit a rosy glow in the afternoon sunlight, and the electric fire on the hearth kept the living room warm and cozy.

I was particularly fond of her husband, Jack. Uncle Jack was a gentle man with a hearty laugh and an off-beat sense of humor. During the war he had worked in Gibraltar for a while and had developed a love of flamenco dancing. When Jose Greco, the greatest flamenco dancer of his day, performed on various television shows, Uncle Jack was always glued to the set. As Jose tapped and postured to the vibrant Spanish rhythms, Uncle Jack would reminisce about Gibraltar and his admiration for the dark-eyed Spanish senoritas; a fact that heartily annoyed Aunt Violet who would snort,

"Oh for heaven's sake, Jack, have you forgotten they don't shave under their arms or wash often enough."

But Uncle Jack would ignore her and lose himself in the flamenco performance, while Aunt Violet would look over at us, roll her eyes, and just shrug her shoulders.

However, on Saturday nights, it would be Aunt Violet's turn. For then Dale Robertson, astride his trusty steed, would gallop across the television set in the popular Western series, "Tales of Wells Fargo." He was a handsome, charismatic character who always triumphed over any number of evil antagonists. And, Aunt Violet thought he was just wonderful.

In preparation for the show, she would go upstairs, fix her hair, and apply fresh lipstick. She would then reemerge, suitably presentable, to sit in her comfortable chair and watch her favorite star. When we teased her about her eccentric behavior, she would laugh along with us and say,

"I know, I know, but it gives me such a lift to get myself fixed up when he comes on." Aunt Violet's admiration of Dale Robertson knew no bounds.

"Och, isn't he lovely," she would say unabashedly. "Did you ever see the likes of him?"

It was really more of a statement than a question, and then it would be Uncle Jack's turn to shake his head. Still, he remained unfazed by Aunt Violet's mini infatuation with this handsome upholder of justice. They both knew that, whether Spanish senoritas, or handsome special agents; their regard for these characters was all just a bit of fantasy that meant nothing in the real world. Uncle Jack was devoted to Aunt Violet, and even years later after she died, he had never even considered remarrying, because, as he flatly declared,

"Your Aunt Violet is irreplaceable."

Uncle Jack worked at the Harland and Wolff shipyards as an electrician. The shipyards were a staple of the Belfast economy, and since the first big steamship, The Venetian, launched in 1860, the yards had turned out a succession of steamships, aircraft carriers and heavy cruisers. At one time they housed the biggest dry dock in the world. One of their most famous ships was the R.M.S. Titanic. Over the years, the shipyards have employed thousands of men, and one of the men who helped build the Titanic was my great-grandfather, David Mackay.

There was an enormous sense of community pride in the fact that such a magnificent vessel had been built in the Belfast Shipyards, and when the word came that the Titanic had gone down, the city was plunged into mourning. Many of the crew and passengers were from Belfast and the surrounding area. The collective shock and grief felt across Northern Ireland is reflected in the newspaper headlines from that time, and it is also recorded in the form of written and recorded reminiscences at the Ulster Folk and Transport Museum.

After the disaster, the city erected a memorial to the ship on the grounds of the same City Hall where, years later, I would often eat my lunch and listen to the band. The Titanic memorial is in the form of a large white statue. It represents the goddess, Thane, who stands as two sea-nymphs at her feet lift a drowned sailor from the sea. The granite pedestal includes a dedication and the names of the men from Northern Ireland who died on board, covering all four sides. It reads:

> ERECTED TO THE IMPERISHABLE MEMORY OF THOSE GALLANT BELFAST MEN WHOSE NAMES ARE HERE INSCRIBED AND WHO LOST THEIR LIVES ON THE 15TH APRIL 1912 BY THE FOUNDERING OF THE BELFAST BUILT R.M.S. TITANIC THROUGH COLLISION WITH AN ICEBERG ON HER MAIDEN VOYAGE FROM SOUTHAMPTON TO NEW YORK.
>
> THEIR DEVOTION TO DUTY AND HEROIC CONDUCT THROUGH WHICH THE LIVES OF MANY OF THOSE ON BOARD WERE SAVED HAVE LEFT A RECORD OF CALM FORTITUDE AND SELF-SACRIFICE WHICH WILL EVER REMAIN AN INSPIRING EXAMPLE TO SUCCEEDING GENERATIONS.
>
> GREATER LOVE HATH NO MAN THAN THIS THAT A MAN LAY DOWN HIS LIFE FOR HIS FRIENDS.

Standing in the City Hall grounds, the statue represents the community pride in having built such a great ship and the sorrow felt at her tragic loss.

As well as the shipyards, the Linen Industry was a major source of employment in Belfast. It had been developed around the time of the American War of Independence when the cotton supplies from the Southern States had dried up. The big linen mills also employed great numbers of people and, for a time, Aunt Violet worked as a seamstress at different factories, although by the time I was visiting her, she had given up her outside jobs. However, she was always sewing or knitting various items that would invariably be given away to family members, and she bought one of the first knitting machines that became available for home use. I think, though, that she just preferred to sit by the fire and knit the old fashioned way—with needles.

She loved babies and for a long time was a foster mother to various homeless little ones. Any baby that was lucky enough to be placed with her would be well fed, cuddled often, and always smelled pleasantly of baby soap and talcum powder.

As time went by, I began to spend more and more time at Aunt Violet's house, and, dreaded going back to Rathcoole.

However, I was fortunate in the fact that Aunt Violet and Uncle Jack were not my only relatives living in Belfast.

Uncle Herbert, daddy's half-brother and his mother, my step grand-mother, also lived near Belfast—in Dundonald. It was just a short walk from the end of the trolley car line to their house in the center of the village.

One Saturday after I moved to Rathcoole, Uncle Herbert picked me up in his little grey Saab and took me on a tour of the city.

As we drove along, I was surprised by the number of empty and ruined sites on our route.

"What happened to all these places?" I asked him.

"Bombed out during the war," was his terse reply.

"But the war was over eleven years ago." I said. "And they're still like that?"

"Well, half the city was destroyed in the air raids." he said. He glanced over at me as though he was wondering if he should go on. Eventually, he must have decided that, at fourteen, I was old enough to hear the details. He took a deep breath before he continued.

"The first raid was on Easter Sunday," he began. "It was a clear full-moon night, so even though all the buildings had black-out blinds, the countryside was lit up by the moonlight." He paused for a moment as though he was picturing it in his mind. The he went on.

"Did you know that the German bombers came up by Strangford Lough and flew over Newtownards on their way to the city?" he said. His voice had an uncharacteristic edge to it, and he paused as if giving me time to let that information sink in.

"Strangford Lough," I exclaimed.

Strangford Lough. The lough along which I had traveled for years on my way up to school in Newtownards!

I tried to imagine the German bombers droning through the night sky over the peaceful waters and the green fields; fields that would have been bathed in silvery moonlight. Could the pilots have seen the white sheep grazing by the narrow winding road that ran alongside the lough? Even though their targets were the shipyards and the city with its manufacturing plants, I wondered if any of them were struck by the beauty of the illuminated countryside. Had any of the pilots suffered a momentary pang as they embarked on their mission of destruction against this tranquil country?

My thoughts branched out and I could almost feel the fear of the people as the bombs began to rein down on Belfast, because I had suddenly remembered that Aunt Violet had once talked about the war, and how during the air raids, she and her sister, Lily, had sat huddled under the stairs, drinking tea and praying for the bombings to stop.

Uncle Herbert's voice brought me back into the present.

"The city just wasn't prepared," he said. "They didn't think Belfast would be a target because the German bombers didn't have that kind of range. But once they captured France, they could take off from the Northern French airfields."

I looked around me at the sunny streets, bustling with afternoon shoppers. I tried to imagine the shops and houses in flames, buildings collapsing, trapping people inside them, and the shipyards that we had just driven past erupting into a raging inferno.

"Not only was half the city destroyed," Uncle Herbert went on. "But over a thousand people were killed; thousands more were injured and thousand left homeless. At one point armies of people were sleeping in the fields. The morgues couldn't handle the bodies, so they were just laid out in the streets."

The bitterness in Uncle Herbert's voice was palpable and I remembered that same tone in Mrs. Johnson's voice when I decided that I wanted to be called *Geri* instead of *Geraldine*. Mrs. Johnson lived at the end of our lane just outside the estate gates and I often dropped in on my way home from school to chat. She was always embroidering linen and cotton tablecloths to be sold in America. She would sit in her chair with the tablecloth spread out over her lap and skeins of colored thread in the basket by her side. She worked quickly, and intricate patters of dainty pink and blue and purple flowers would magically materialize across the crisp white cloth.

"I can't call you *Geri,*" she declared, in tone that I had never heard her use before. She never actually called me Geraldine.

She always managed to drop the "d" and the word came out as Geraline.

I looked at her in surprise.

"Why not?" I asked

"That's what we called the Germans," she explained. "*Gerries.*" "And I remember seeing the sky lit up red, even from this far away when the city was on fire during the bombings." She shook her head emphatically. "No, you will never be *Geri* to me."

The edge in her voice warned me never to broach the subject again.

Uncle Herbert's voice interrupted my thoughts.

"The Doodlebugs were the worst," he said. "Because when the engine stopped, that's when you knew it was coming down."

I had heard about the Doodlebugs and I could not imagine how frightening it must have been to hear the engine of a self-propelled five-hundred-pound bomb sputter, and then cut out, and know that when it landed it could demolish an entire block of houses."

"They bombed the Water Works first," Uncle Herbert continued. "Because that way there wouldn't be enough water pressure to put out the fires. But the firemen," he exclaimed. "They were the heroes. They came from all over—even from Dublin, a hundred miles away. They were all volunteers. They drove here, even though they couldn't use their running lights because of the blackout. Instead, they used the moonlight and followed the overhead telephone wires as a guide."

He shook his head.

"It was such a terrible time," he went on. All those people dead, all those little children." His voice trailed off. He looked across at me, and I think he remember that I had just lost my father and my little sister, and suddenly regretted elaborating on the horrors of war. Also, I think he realized that it was all a bit much for a fourteen year old girl to take in.

However, he did not know that my mind had already slid away from the mental images of death and destruction. I was remembering Errol Flynn, the swashbuckling movie star, and how I had once heard that his father, a Professor of Biology who lectured at Queens University, had brought bottles of rum to the rescue workers after the raids. And then, images of the sword-wielding

Errol, swinging across the screen rescuing maidens in distress, replaced all the gloomy thoughts of war.

I think Uncle Herbert sensed that he had lost my attention.

He sighed.

"Ah well," he said. "Sure it's a better day now."

Uncle Herbert was very good to me. He took me to all the Christmas shows, and for drives around the countryside. I think Daddy was his favorite brother, and I believe he missed visiting us at the estate. He was a bachelor who did not marry until later in life. Perhaps he did well to wait, for when he did eventually marry, he and his lovely wife Irene had a very happy marriage.

He worked as a manager at Goodyear Tires. The company was just a couple of streets over from Hamilton's Ford Dealers where I worked, and it was an easy walk over if I wanted to see him.

Uncle Herbert and Aunt Violet provided comfort as I struggled with my grief at loosing Daddy, Ruth, my friends, and my beloved home.

However, I was still desperately lonely.

CHAPTER SEVENTEEN

Escape from Rathcoole

The last time my husband and I went home, we stayed at one of the lodge houses inside the walled estate. This particular lodge is on the north side of the estate next to the village and the seashore.

One evening, acting on a sudden impulse, I said to my husband "Let's go and see my old house."

We could easily have driven out of the iron gates and around the estate to my former home; however I had an overwhelming desire to retrace my steps from childhood.

When I told my husband how I felt, he said, "All right, we can walk up there and just take our time."

So, as I had done almost every day while growing up, we strolled along the tree lined road, over the old stone bridge, past the Manor House, and around the rhododendron lined avenue. By the time we emerged through the tall gates on the south side of the estate, dusk was falling and a chill had descended on the night air.

Suddenly I was ten years old again.

It was a December evening and I was coming home from the village. As I rounded the corner, walked through the estate gates and looked up towards my house, I was transfixed by what appeared to be a mirage of twinkling colored lights at the top of our lane. As I came closer, I realized that the lights were emanating from our house—from a Christmas tree in our sitting room window.

I went into the house where my father had just finished setting up and decorating a beautifully-proportioned Christmas tree. The pungent smell of pine filled the cold, unheated room, and the glittering red and yellow and green lights, reflecting off our polished piano, transforming the room into Christmas magic.

I was enchanted.

We never had a tree and there was never any fuss made over Christmas. We would go to church and get a present—usually a jigsaw puzzle or a pen and a book, and I don't remember having visitors come to our house to celebrate the season.

In retrospect, the appearance of the Christmas tree was indicative of the relationship my sister and I had with our father. He tried to give to us, without ever giving of himself. He presented the tree, but he did not provide us with the anticipation, or share the decoration, of it with us. He did not tell us he planned to have a tree, and we did not decorate it together. To do those things would have meant physical and emotional interaction. I suppose in his own way he was trying to make up for Aunt Sally leaving. He loved us but he was emotionally detached. I think he just had too many profound losses in his life to risk being vulnerable again.

Because my sister and I were used to Daddy being physically present, while emotionally apart, it never occurred to us to question the way the tree had just suddenly appeared in our sitting room.

At the time, it didn't matter. The important thing was that I loved the tree, and that first sight of it has become a magical moment, stored forever in some protected corner of my memory. And I can still conjure up the excitement I felt that entire Christmas season each time I walked up the lane, through the dark December night towards those magical twinkling lights.

I look back now and feel grateful to my father, because despite his inability to overtly show his love, he had tried, in his own way, to give his young daughters something that was truly special.

Their very own Christmas tree.

In the years after Daddy and Ruth died, I dreaded the Christmas season; for it was then that my feeling of loss and loneliness became almost unbearable. I think my stepmother must have felt the same way. However, by that time I had made the decision never to become close to anyone again. That was to be my defense. We all have our own particular ways of coping with sorrow. For my stepmother it was to anesthetize her pain with religion.

It seems strange to me now that her particular sect, which focused on the threat of Hellfire and Brimstone, would be a comfort. It declared, in the most violent terms, that we are all miserable sinners, and that only through strict adherence to its particular interpretation of the scriptures could one find salvation. It emphasized the image of Hell as a dreadful place, and I wonder why she had originally been drawn to a religion that promoted fear, not kindness and hope.

It espoused a doctrine of condemnation and suffering, and I realize now how psychologically damaging these message were to me—a fourteen year old girl who was actively mourning the loss of both her parents, her two sisters and her beloved home.

As time went by, my stepmother became more and more immersed in her bible and her Plymouth Brethren meetings. On one level, I could almost understand why she became increasingly enveloped in religion. After all, she was in her early forties, had only been married for three years, and had already lost her husband and her little daughter. I think it was the belief that she would one day be with Daddy and Ruth again that kept her going.

What I did not like was the fact that she began encouraging me to join her particular religion.

I resented the fact that I was being pressured into attending her Plymouth Brethren meetings. I already attended the Church of Ireland, so it was not as though I was some type of heathen who needed to be converted. Besides, I was used to my own established church. It was a church where the minister wore robes. A church where we sang hymns dedicated to sailors and fishermen; where, each Sunday, Lord Dunleath would duly mount the steps to the altar to read the designated scriptures for the week. It was a church that was joyfully decorated with sheaves of wheat, and baskets of fruit and vegetables at the annual Harvest Thanksgiving service. It had organ music that soared to the rafters and a choir that sang with gusto. My church had marble pillars, exquisite stained glass windows, and bells that pealed out across the countryside calling the faithful to Sunday services. It was an environment that evoked a feeling of spirituality.

Coming from this background, the Plymouth Brethren service, which was held in a stark meeting room, seemed like an unsuitable and unacceptable place to talk about God. Strangely enough, the fact that Jesus was a simple man who preached in all types of settings, and whose disciples came from humble origins, did not alter my opinion that worship should be theatrical and glorious.

As time went by, my stepmother began to pressure me into attending her meetings on Tuesday and Thursday nights every week. I can only say that they were terrible affairs that frightened the life out of me, and I eventually began to have nightmares.

The preacher, a beefy, middle aged man, would stand and wave his bible about in the air while shouting at the congregation.

"Everyone who doesn't abide by the scriptures is destined for Hell. Women who paint their faces and flirt with men are like Jezebel." At this point, he would take a deep breath and wind up to continue the tirade.

"These women! These terrible women! They will end up screaming for mercy in the everlasting fire as the flames engulf their sinful bodies."

Perhaps this particular condemnation sticks in my mind because the preacher was glaring at me—the youngest person in the congregation. Why was he singling me out to be the recipient of this onslaught? Did he know that I had been going without lunch, so that I could save my lunch money to buy lipstick to wear when I was safely far away at Aunt Violet's house? Did he know that I had a crush on Martin Caldwell and was trying to build up the nerve to flirt with him?

I began to have throbbing headaches and bad dreams. As the nightmares intensified, I went to the minister at the Church of Ireland where I attended services. He was a quite a young man with a large shock of black hair, and a lovely cultured Dublin accent. He was outgoing and had a good rapport with the congregation. Unlike the self-proclaimed preacher at my stepmothers' meetings, he had a Doctorate in Divinity and was trained in dealing with the psychological wellbeing of his flock.

He said, "Tell her you have to stop going there. Tell her about your bad dreams. If she still keeps asking you to accompany her, I will go and tell her in no uncertain terms that you already belong to an established church, and that going to her meetings is making you ill."

I think that as soon as my stepmother realized that I had talked to my own minister about her, and that he was in my corner, she conceded that she had lost the battle for my conversion to her sect. Thankfully, she never asked me to go with her again.

However, the conservative views espoused by her religion did spill over me in other areas.

Living surrounded by the Old Folk's Cottages made it impossible for me to leave the house without being observed by their inhabitants. Most of these old age pensioners were in poor health, and for the most part, house-bound. It seemed to me that their primary occupation was to sit, peering out of their windows waiting for something of external interest to occur. In this day and age, they would be watching television or exploring the Internet. It must have been hard to face each day, suffering as they did, from the various physical impairments that come with aging. Outside of the radio, they had few sources of diversion or entertainment. However, since they reported every aspect of my deportment to my step-mother, I find it hard, even now, not to feel angry at having been subjected to that constant, judgmental scrutiny.

When my stepmother confronted me about going out wearing slacks, or once, actually holding hands with my boyfriend, Martin Caldwell as we walked out to the main road to catch the bus, I listened in silence.

"It's just not the proper thing to so," she would emphatically. "And I don't want you to do it again."

I knew that, had I repeated these (and other benign) offences again, our old-fashioned, elderly neighbors would have lost no time in making sure my stepmother was made aware of my non-compliance.

I never tried to defend myself or plead my case. All I ever did was to mumble some type of vague, conciliatory answer.

I had not developed the inner sense of self that comes with a strong family connection. That feeling of belonging and support had eroded when Aunt Sally left us, and had then deepened when my father died.

In short, I never felt as though I had any individual rights, and because of stepmother's restrictive dictates, it was as though I had lost control over my own life. Her directives created a wedge between us that widened as time went by.

I should have been grateful to her for giving me a home when, as far as I knew, none of my relatives had offered to take me in, however I was consumed with homesickness for Ballywalter, the estate and my friends. After Aunt Sally left, my environment had become like a parent to me. I was embraced by it and it nurtured me. I missed the fields and the woods, the sea and the village as much as I missed my father. I understand why the North American Indians referred to their environment as "Mother Earth," and why they fought so fiercely to retain their lands. To lose the environment, with which one has a profound affinity, is like losing a part of oneself.

I never expressed any of this to my stepmother. She simply would not have understood how staying on the estate and the farm would have sustained me the way her religion nurtured her in our time of grief.

Eventually, an irreversible chasm developed between us.

In my endeavors to escape from Rathcoole, I sometimes went to Dundonald to visit my step-grandmother. Vivi and I called her "Finaghy Granny," because when we were growing up she lived in the Finaghy region of Belfast. I only remember going there once as a child. Uncle Stanley, her youngest son, had driven down to Ballywalter in his little red convertible sports car and transported us up to her house for the day.

I was fascinated by her house. The door bell was hooked to a series of chimes in the hall, and when the button was pressed resonant peals reverberated throughout the house. She had a magnificent china cabinet filled with figurines, tiny crystal ornaments and painted ceramics, and all the wooden surfaces of her furniture were so polished that I could actually see my reflection in them.

By the time I was living in Rathcoole, Finaghy Granny had moved from the Belfast house to her two-storied home in Dundonald where she lived with my Uncle Herbert. She was a tiny woman who always dressed in severe Widow's Black and old-fashioned, laced-up shoes. She had a long, thin face that was set in a perpetual scowl, and her grey hair was scraped back into a large bun at the nape of her neck. I always thought that if you put a pointed, wide-brimmed, black hat on her head, and draped a black cloak around her shoulders, she could have been physically transformed into the type of witch who always populated children's fairy tales. I find it chilling to think that, back then, she was not much older that I am today.

I once tried to give her a mental make-over, dying her hair light brown, applying a little subtle makeup to her chalk white face and dressing her in trendy clothes. It never seemed to make the transformation I was hoping for. Her strong personality and distinctive appearance defied any mental adjustments I tried to make to soften her look.

Despite her diminutive size, she had raised three strapping sons in a time when there were no modern conveniences, and when being a mother and a housewife meant endless work that often bordered on drudgery.

I didn't go to her house just to escape from Rathcoole. I also went because my strong need for family, no matter how peripheral; transcended the fact that she had been the second wife to my grandfather who had died four years before I was born. Besides, her son, my Uncle Herbert, even though he was my half-uncle, was as real an uncle as if he had been my father's full brother.

Uncle Herbert was never there on Sunday afternoons when I visited, and I think Finaghy Granny was glad of my company. She was always nice to me, and gave me her full attention.

Before long, she would bring me into the kitchen and give me afternoon tea. She would produce cakes of soda and wheat bread that she had baked on Saturday, slice them up and smother them with butter and jam and pour me a china cup of tea from her large country-cottage tea pot.

Her conversation sometimes revolved around how lonely she was, and how she wished Uncle Herbert would spend more time at home. However, she was always interested in what I had to say.

"What have you been doing with yourself all week?" she would ask, then listen patiently as I talked about work and the Saturday night dance.

"Mary doesn't know you're dancing, does she?" she once asked me.

Everybody in the family, on both sides, knew that my stepmother was so straight-laced that she even thought going to the movies was sinful. Finaghy Granny knew that she would have been horrified if she knew that I was actually dancing, however since I spent every Saturday night at Aunt Violet's house, my stepmother had no idea of where I was going or what I was doing.

"No," I replied.

"Well you'd better not let her find out, or she'll be having a conniption, and forbid you to do that too," was Finaghy Granny's wry comment.

Uncle Herbert was the son who lived with her. I think she was the reason he stayed single for so long. However, I think it turned out to be an advantage because he eventually met and married the sweet-natured Irene in what turned out to be a long and happy union. Still, even then, he took care of Finaghy Granny, and it was because of his attentiveness that even though she lived well into her nineties, she was able to stay in her Dundonald house until she died.

It was my Uncle Herbert who, monitoring the deteriorating situation between my stepmother and myself, and realizing that an irreversible rift had developed between us, decided to do something about my predicament. He knew I was trying to avoid my stepmother as much as possible, only coming home to the house when I knew she would be gone, and spending every weekend I could at Aunt Violet's house. He knew how religious and restrictive she had become, and he suspected how unhappy and desperate I felt. Finally, resolving to take matters into his own hands, he made the decision to write to my Uncle Sam in America. In his letter, he described my predicament, and suggested that Uncle Sam offer to bring me to America.

It was a fateful act that changed my life forever.

A short time later, I received a letter from my Uncle in Massachusetts inviting me to come and live with him.

I was ecstatic. I had been offered a way out.

I was about to escape from Rathcoole.

I was going to America.

CHAPTER EIGHTEEN

Going To America

I think that all immigrants who come to America initially suffer from some form of culture shock.

I was no exception.

I was used to walking, riding my bicycle or taking the bus. To my astonishment, in the rural area outside Boston where my Uncle lived, everyone seemed to own a car, and cars were used for even the shortest of trips. People just did not walk everywhere the way they did at home.

Eating became a new experience. I had never seen an ear of Indian corn, heard of peanut butter or tasted blueberry pie. Restaurants served enormous portions of food, and picnics were a staple of summer life.

I was introduced to "the shower." I was amazed by this contraption, where, instead of taking a bath, one would stand in the tub and wash oneself with water that sprayed out of a pipe in the wall.

I thought that whoever invented the drive-In theater was a genius. Imagine being able to watch a movie in your car. At home, the theaters had ashtrays attached to the backs of the seats. With so many patrons using them, the air was sometimes so heavy with blue-grey smoke that the images on the screen would appear hazy. So, the idea of being able to sit and watch a movie in comfort and privacy seemed almost decadent.

Yet, perhaps one of my most vivid experiences was to come downstairs in my uncle's house the morning after I arrived, and to hear a catchy tune being sung on the radio.

It was a jingle for a coffee advertisement.

You get forty three beans
In every cup—of Nescafe

The cheery chorus filled the kitchen, and used as I was to only hearing the semi-classical music and the news on the BBC, I remember the shock I felt at the idea of at having product promotions piped into the home environment—especially first thing in the morning.

All of these new experiences made me wonder what it must have been like for those early immigrants for whom America was a great unknown. In contrast, I was coming in a modern time to a welcoming home. Also, thanks to my schooling (and Hollywood), I had general knowledge of the country, and the advantage of speaking the same language.

However, I am sure of one thing that all immigrants, young and old, have had in common.

Hope for a new and promising, life.

In America.

After I arrived in America, I received some startling information. My Uncle Sam's wife, Marie, told me that, after my father died, my uncle had written to my stepmother offering to bring Vivi and myself to America to live with them.

My stepmother had never told me about the invitation.

Instead, she wrote back saying that she could on no account "give me up."

"Those were your stepmother's exact words," my aunt said.

I was astonished.

However, in retrospect, I actually think that my stepmother's refusal, and her secrecy surrounding the offer was based on the fact that she had become genuinely fond of me, and also because she viewed me as her last, closest link to Daddy. I suspect she did not tell Vivi as my sister was poised to begin her nurses training at Belfast City Hospital. During the three-year training period, she was required to live with the other student nurses at the hospital dormitories. Besides had she told Vivi, I would have found out about Uncle Sam's letter and might have opted to go to America.

What my stepmother did not realize was that I do not think either of us would have taken Uncle Sam up on his offer. Vivi had already decided on medicine as a career, and I was actively mourning the loss of my home at the estate. At least Rathcoole was only twenty-six miles away from Ballywalter, and the idea of being 3,000 miles away would have been unthinkable. By living at Rathcoole, I would still be able to regularly return to Ballywalter, Hilary's house and the Estate. That would have been impossible had I gone to America. However, this latest offer was addressed directly to me, and I had just spent four lonely, miserable years in that sad, empty house in Rathcoole.

I jumped at the chance to belong to a real family.

I was now eighteen and I knew that this decision was mine alone to make. With both my Uncles involved, my stepmother would have no choice but to acquiesce to their decision. In all honesty, considering our estranged relationship, perhaps it was also a relief for her to see me go.

I wrote back to my Uncle, thanking him for his offer, and accepting his invitation.

When he received my letter, he immediately set about arranging immigration status for me. He applied to the American Embassy requesting all the necessary documents required to bring me into America as a legal alien. He hired a lawyer to fill out the paperwork, and to prepare financial statements that would prove his ability to support me for the first year of my stay. These papers were then submitted to the American Embassy in Belfast. After the application was approved, I had to wait for an opening in the immigration quota from the United Kingdom.

It was a year before I was given a date to enter the United States.

That last year I had spent waiting to go to America was a strange one. I still visited my sister at the hospital. Sometimes, when she was on night duty, I would visit her on the ward, helping her make the tea. She had quite a lot of patients to take care of by herself. She not only had to administer the medications, she was also in charge of the evening snacks. I used to go around giving out cups of tea to the patients who were eligible for evening refreshments. I suppose I was really an unauthorized volunteer, however my sister did not have a lot of time off and this was my way of staying in touch with her.

A few months before I left, I took a job at the Elk Inn. It was conveniently situated at the end of the trolley line in Dundonald, not far from my Finaghy Granny's house. I worked in the family bar on Friday and Saturday nights. Since I was staying with Aunt Violet's on the weekend, my secret was safe from my stepmother. I told Uncle Herbert about my new venture and he came to the bar one Saturday night, no doubt to check up on the place and to determine that it was respectable. He need not have worried as it was frequented by the same few couples each week and, unlike the upstairs bar, was never busy. I don't think he was keen on the idea of me working there. In the multi-level class system at home, I believe he felt that no member of our family should be tending bar.

I just wanted to make some extra money to buy clothes to take to America.

I wrote to Hilary to tell her about my impending adventure. I did not get down to Ballywalter very much any more as I was working much of the time. I think I deliberately avoided going there before I left. It would have been like leaving it all over again, and that kind of pain would have dampened the enthusiasm I had for my voyage to America.

When a slot opened in the immigration quota from the United Kingdom, my uncle arranged for a passage for me on the Furness Withey Shipping Line. The ship sailed out of Liverpool, England to Boston, with stops in St. John, Newfoundland and Halifax, Nova Scotia. I was to take the night ferry from Belfast to Liverpool, and the following day board the ship to America.

My goodbye to my stepmother was strained. She was polite; however I confess that by that time, I was so alienated from her, that my goodbye to her was barely civil. It has taken a long time for me to be able to look back with perspective on our relationship, and I now regret that I never went to see her when I went back home for visits. I think she was well-intentioned; however she had been thrust into a situation that she was ill equipped to handle. I don't think my father realized the potentially negative ramifications of creating a stepmother for Vivi and myself. I believe he thought it his duty to provide a mature, female presence who would cook and clean, and create a stable home life for us.

However, even after Mary came to live with us, he was often gone in the evening, and once when she went to visit her sister for a few days, I remember seeing a note to her written on the back of an envelope and left in plain sight on the kitchen table.

It said, "Welcome home, Bill."

"Welcome home." But why was he not there to welcome her home in person. After all she had been gone for three days. He was a good man, always doing electrical jobs for the surrounding farmers, but he was just not family material. I think he was a bit of a gypsy at heart, only happy when he was roaming around the country on his motor cycle.

He did make an exception on Sunday evenings. When she went to her meeting in the village, he would sit smoking his pipe, rocking Ruth's pram with one foot while he read a book and listened to the Sunday night classical concert on the radio.

I do think that my stepmother was a victim. She was a victim of circumstances, a victim of tragedy, a victim of her own religion, and ultimately a victim of her own inability to be flexible. I was happy to be leaving her. Those four years spent in that unhappy house in Rathcoole only deepened the scar created by never knowing my mother or my sister, Patricia, by having Aunt Sally abruptly abandon us, by Daddy and Ruth dying, and by losing my beloved home at the estate.

After I said goodbye to my stepmother, I never saw her again.

When I left Belfast on the night ferry, my sister and Aunt Violet went with me. We spent the next day in Liverpool waiting to until it was time for me to board the ship to America. I confess that I have almost no recollection of the day. I do know that I spent it in tears, although the terrible emptiness I felt at leaving home, my sister and my aunt was somewhat offset by the excitement of the hustle and bustle as I boarded the ship. At one point during the day, Vivi and I had our picture taken together. In it, my face is swollen from crying, and my sister's long fair hair, released from underneath her usual nurses' cap, is uncharacteristically tumbling down her back. I don't know what happened to the picture—it vanished long ago.

The passenger ship I came across the Atlantic on was absolutely nothing like the liners that cross the oceans today. It was a bare bones form of travel. I suspect that the shipping company made most of its money from transporting cargo as there were only about sixty or seventy passengers on board.

The passengers were an eclectic bunch. There were two Hispanic college students from Los Angeles who had been back-packing around Europe, a doctor and his wife, and also a nurse, who were immigrating. There was a missionary couple returning from Africa. They had six children all under the age of twelve. There were also a couple of business types and a few people on holiday.

I shared a cabin with a lady whom I judged to be around forty. When I first entered the cabin, she was lying on one of the bunks. She sat up and looked over at me.

"What's your name?" she asked. I told her my name.

"Well, Geraldine," she said, "I have very bad nerves so noises bother me, and I'm going to need peace and quiet."

She then proceeded to spend most of the voyage in her bunk with the curtains draw. I never once saw her in the dining room so someone must have brought her meals to the cabin. The other occupant was a girl of about twenty who disappeared in the morning and then reappeared in the evening . . . I never did find out where she went all day. It wasn't a big ship and there was only one small lounge on the upper deck with a 180 degree view of the front of the ship. It had a piano, a few books and some magazines. Passengers were left to their own devices. I spent most of my time wandering around the deck and talking to the backpackers and whatever crew members happened to be on the deck at the time.

The dining hall had ten tables . . . actually they were more like benches that came out from the wall, and because this ship was not stabilized like the passenger ships today, the three sides of the tables that protruded from the wall also had rims that lifted up, so that in a storm the dishes wouldn't slide off, and break on the floor. I was across from an old couple that sat grey-haired and hunched over their food. They didn't talk, and they never looked at anybody. I never saw them in the lounge either, so I think they only left their cabins to have their silent meals

On the third day out we ran headlong into one of those fierce North Atlantic, spring storms. The passengers were forbidden to go out on the deck, and I spend the day up in the lounge listening to the ship groan and creak, and watching the bow as it plunged and reared forward through the heaving sea. At the low point, the sea was actually crashing over the deck. Occasionally, a crew member, struggling against the wind, would inch his way from one side of the ship to the other, clinging hand over hand to one of the ropes that had been strung across the deck when the storm began. I found it exhilarating because, in my youthful ignorance, it simply never occurred to me that at any time a rogue wave could have swamped and capsized us, a thousand miles out from land. The storm raged for two days until we sailed into calmer waters.

Two days from Boston, our destination, the ship officers held a dance. One of them had a record player and we all congregated in a room down below the top deck. We were coming to the end of the voyage, and everyone was excited at the knowledge that we would soon be in America. It was all very festive, and apart from the missionaries, the old folk and the nervous lady, all of the passengers went to the dance. We did all the country dances, and then . . . . in the middle of the Gay Gordons, the doctor's wife, who was as tall as I am, heavily pregnant, and wearing stiletto heels, lost her balance and her stiletto heel, with her full weight behind it, rammed down on the top of my foot. I sank to the floor doubled up in pain.

By the morning my foot and a third of my leg was swollen to twice its size and badly bruised. The ship's doctor determined that it was not broken and wrapped it up in bandages.

My foot and my leg was extremely painful, however the next day, I temporarily forgot the discomfort when, suddenly, the coast of America came into view. Everyone was out on deck marveling at the rocky coast off in the distance and the seemingly never-ending dark-green forests of the state of Maine as we moved on toward our destination, Boston, Massachusetts.

When the ship arrived in Boston, what a sight I was coming down the gangplank, with my leg swathed in thick, white bandages, limping heavily, and carrying my two suitcases.

My aunt and uncle were on the dock waiting for me. For some time, I had been quite nervous at the idea of meeting them. What if they did not like me? What if I could not fit in?

I need not have worried.

My uncle came towards me and his first words were.

"You look just like your mother." He paused and smiled at me. "I really liked her."

He could not have chosen a better greeting. In those two sentences, he expressed the affection and acceptance that I had craved since Aunt Sally left.

It was the best welcome I could have received as I started my new and exciting life.

In America.

EPILOGUE

As a child, I was addicted to happy endings.

I was delighted that Cinderella was finally whisked away from her dreary existence by the handsome Prince; that the steady tortoise finished the race before the derisive hare; and that the ugly ducking finally turned into a beautiful swan.

Fortunately as children, we do not have the perspective to suspect that standard "Happily ever after" ending might be problematic. Were Cinderella and the prince really able to develop the compatibility necessary in sustaining a long-term relationship? Could the plodding tortoise have won the race had the hare not been overconfident? And, would the beautiful swan be happy living his life without friends of his own species?

Then as we grow up, we realize that real life endings are never quite that tidy. On the surface it might seem that in coming to America I should have been instantly happy. However, although my uncle and aunt were kind to me, I still felt a pervasive sense of loss and loneliness, which combined with a shaky identity, was deep-seated and not easily eradicated.

Awed by the diversity and strangeness of this exotic land, I never felt completely comfortable in this different culture although I was desperate to fit in and be accepted.

Yet happily in many ways, America has indeed been my salvation, and living here has allowed me a fresh perspective on my early life. There is an energy and sense of hope in the U.S. that is not always felt in the more established European countries. America is an exciting place to live and it has always been open and welcoming to me. As soon as I was able, I became a naturalized citizen.

Like most people, my life has consisted of ups and downs, and it has often been a struggle to move beyond the effect of childhood bereavements. Since coming to America, Aunt Violet, Uncle Jack and Uncle Hebert have passed on. Uncle Sam, who so generously brought me to this country, and my Uncle Vivian in Australia, who wrote me voluminous letters in response to my requests for information about my father's childhood, are no longer with us.

And although at some deep level, I have spent my life in perpetual mourning, I realize in writing this book that we never really lose the people we love. Memories of my family poured out onto the pages. Sometimes the recollections were painful, but in the long run, therapeutic.

As I write this, I am surrounded by my present-day family—my husband, Gordon, my daughters, Kathleen and Tara, my sons-in-law, Terry and Mitch, and my grandchildren, Kaitlyn and Ian. We are healthy, compatible and appreciate each other. I am in regular contact with my sister, Vivienne, who now lives in England, and we visit each other almost every year.

I recently heard that "gratitude" is the secret to happiness, and in taking stock of my life, I realize that I have indeed a lot to be thankful for. I was fortunate to have peripheral family and friends who always stepped in to ease the voids; to have been given a chance for a new beginning in a country of opportunity; and to have finally found the close family connection I have always craved.

Could this be my happy ending?

I believe so.

I love happy endings.

CPSIA information can be obtained
at www.ICGtesting.com
Printed in the USA
LVHW090704140221
679244LV00046B/28/J